A PLUME BOOK

THE BUSINESS OF BULLSHIT

GRAHAM EDMONDS has over twenty-five years' experience of being on the receiving end of office bullshit. He lives in the UK.

The Business
of Bullshit

A HUMOROUS GUIDE TO
THE SPIN, HYPE, AND PRETENSE
OF THE MODERN WORLD

Graham Edmonds

A PLUME BOOK

PLUME
Published by Penguin Group
Penguin Group (USA) Inc., 375 Hudson Street, New York, New York 10014, U.S.A.
Penguin Group (Canada), 90 Eglinton Avenue East, Suite 700, Toronto, Ontario,
Canada M4P 2Y3 (a division of Pearson Penguin Canada Inc.)
Penguin Books Ltd., 80 Strand, London WC2R 0RL, England
Penguin Ireland, 25 St. Stephen's Green, Dublin 2, Ireland (a division of Penguin
Books Ltd.)
Penguin Group (Australia), 250 Camberwell Road, Camberwell, Victoria 3124,
Australia (a division of Pearson Australia Group Pty. Ltd.)
Penguin Books India Pvt. Ltd., 11 Community Centre, Panchsheel Park,
New Delhi – 110 017, India
Penguin Books (NZ), cnr Airborne and Rosedale Roads, Albany, Auckland 1310,
New Zealand (a division of Pearson New Zealand Ltd.)
Penguin Books (South Africa) (Pty.) Ltd., 24 Sturdee Avenue, Rosebank,
Johannesburg 2196, South Africa

Penguin Books Ltd., Registered Offices: 80 Strand, London WC2R 0RL, England

First published by Plume, a member of Penguin Group (USA) Inc.

First Printing, June 2006
10 9 8 7 6 5 4 3 2 1

 REGISTERED TRADEMARK—MARCA REGISTRADA

LIBRARY OF CONGRESS CATALOGING-IN-PUBLICATION DATA

Edmonds, Graham, 1958–
    The business of bullshit : a humorous guide to the spin, hype, and pretense of the
    modern world / Graham Edmonds.
        p.   cm.
ISBN 0-452-28733-2
1. Work—Humor. 2. Interpersonal relations—Humor. I. Title.
PN6231.W644E36 2006
818'.602—dc22

                    2006001249

Printed in the United States of America
Set in Palatino

To Michaela, for all that matters

ACKNOWLEDGMENTS

Here are just a few words of gratitude . . .

I'd particularly like to thank Paul Torjussen of Southbank and Emily Haynes at Plume for their backing, encouragement, and large checks . . . when they arrive.

My thanks also to all those people and colleagues who suggested many of the terms that appear in this book; everyone seems to have a favorite.

Thanks in particular to the now-expelled management at my previous to last company, who were so full of it.

A very big thank-you also goes to Charles Powiesnik, without whom this book would not have been written.

CONTENTS

Acknowledgments   vii

Introduction   xi

1. Bullshitters and Fakes: Recognized Behaviors   1

2. Leaders and Managers   7

3. War, Battles, Fighting, and Guns   33

4. Excuses, Disasters, and Why It All Went Wrong   41

5. Politics, PR, and Spin   57

6. Business Guru Speak   65

7. Consultant Bullshit   81

8. Marketing and Advertising   87

9. Human Resources and People   109

10. Planes, Trains, and Automobiles   127

11. Sporting Bullshit and Clichés   133

x   *Contents*

12. Finance and Accounting   143

13. I.T. Bullshit   161

14. Acronyms   167

15. The Weird and Wonderful   179

16. Playing Hooky   187

The Last Word   191

INTRODUCTION

Welcome to *The Business of Bullshit*. It's the book that lifts the lid on all the bullshit you hear and see around you, especially in the workplace.

We have extended our bullshit detectors, scouring offices from around the world for the best bullshit words and phrases; we've even looked at the ways bullshit is applied in warfare, sports, and music.

The English language evolves constantly, especially in the United States, and office culture, with its atmosphere of competitiveness and opportunity for advancement by bullshit, is a prime place for new words, phrases, metaphors, and euphemisms.

The type of bullshit we're covering in this book is largely corporate and has to do with fakery and the attempt to put one over on a competitor to gain favor or to impress.

To the consummate company bullshitter, it's a way of life; he or she is out to impress all the time. These people want to look good and to use language to make others appear ineffective. This is not about accuracy and fair play, or even good business.

It's often amazing to see what bullshitters get away with; their use of language combined with sheer cheek is fascinating to the observer—unless you are on the receiving end, of course.

The language of bullshit can play a positive role too; it can take the aggression out of situations, and it has provided the surreal comedy from which this book has grown.

This book is divided into sections that reflect company departments and activities such as conferences and recruitment, and each comes with a glossary of terms and explanations of how the office bullshitter uses them. Plus there's a "bullshit bingo" card for you to take to meetings.

We've also included some fun cards on clichés, sports, conference music, and politics.

Everyone who has ever worked in an office has used bullshit at some time during the workday, and we all know those people who live by bullshit. This book is dedicated to them, and long may they continue to entertain us—just as long as they don't undermine us.

So eyes down . . .

BULLSHIT BINGO—The Classics

ON MESSAGE	DUCKS IN A ROW	ENGAGE	DIS-CONNECT	ON THE MAP	JOINED-UP THINKING	MAKE IT WORK	BACK TO BASICS	LEVEL PLAYING FIELD	CHERRY PICK
ENERGY	LOW-HANGING FRUIT	PARK IT	FOCUS	TEMPLATE	BIG PICTURE	GO FOR IT	LAND MINES	WIN HEARTS AND MINDS	CHECK THE BOXES
OFFLINE	GAME PLAN	WIN-WIN	LEARN-INGS	FAST TRACK	STRA-TEGIC	LEARNING CURVE	CHANGE MANAGE	TOUCH BASE	OUTCOME
BENCH-MARK	BALL PARK	PRO-ACTIVE, NOT REACTIVE	CONNECT	BRAIN-STORM	FLIGHT PATH	THE BOTTOM LINE	COOKING WITH GAS	CUS-TOMER DRIVEN	PROCESS
GO THE EXTRA MILE	AT THE END OF THE DAY	FEEDBACK	SCOPE	ROCKET SCIENCE	BARRIER	THINK OUTSIDE THE BOX	CLIENT-FOCUSED	CUS-TOMER FOCUSED	MOVE THE GOAL POSTS
EMPOWER	FRAME-WORK	RESULTS-DRIVEN	BEST PRACTICE	SYNERGY	QUALITY	SKILL SET	MINDSET	ACTION	BASKET CASE

How to play: Simply check off 6 words in one meeting and shout out BINGO!

1. Bullshitters and Fakes: Recognized Behaviors

Dressing up is inevitably a substitute for good ideas. It is no coincidence that technically inept business types are known as "suits."

—Paul Graham

Some of the best bullshitters and fakes appear to take on the persona of the company they work for, seamlessly moving from job to job and often getting large payoffs as they are found out, often making a lot of money in the process. Companies are often too embarrassed to admit their mistakes in employing these people.

Bullshitting is an art. It's all about getting noticed. Watching the way skilled bullshitters align themselves to make the most of their position is pretty impressive, even though you may not approve. Here are some of the typical tricks of the trade.

"Accidentally" Running into the Boss

It's important to know the boss's schedule; bumping into them in the corridor, elevator, restroom, or by the coffee machine is a good way to get attention.

Acting Important

A real skill, it involves wearing culturally correct clothes, knowing what to say in meetings without actually committing to anything, using the right body language to suggest power, all with an attitude that looks completely confident. It involves walking with purpose, talking loudly, and acting in a seemingly very earnest way.

Asking a Question While Knowing the Answer, to Increase Credibility and Profile

Sometimes when this is very cleverly done, the question will be one that enables the boss to shine, allowing the questioner to bask in the reflected glory and to be thought of by the boss in a more positive light.

Being Seen Around the Office

An important prerequisite for anyone who wants to get ahead, being seen is a must for any attention seeker and go-getter. Turning up early when they know it will be noticed or working late when they know the boss is there. Even when not in the office, the best fakes will leave a familiar jacket or bag strategically placed so that it gives the impression that they're around somewhere.

Blaming Ex-colleagues

When someone leaves the company, the office fake will arrange it so that his or her own mistakes can be attributed to the one who left. Those returning to a company they have previously left should be aware.

Business Dress

The best company bullshitters are not necessarily the smartest in the office; they are the ones who dress most like the boss. Alignment by fashion.

Claiming Credit for the Work of Others

A classic tactic and one regularly practiced by unscrupulous bosses everywhere, claiming credit for the work of others requires skill in lying outrageously, barefaced cheek, plausibility, and the ability to keep a straight face as others react when they realize what is going on.

Clapping

A good way to get attention is to clap with hollowed hands; it's louder and sounds more appreciative.

Copying in Select Important People on Memos and E-mails

This is really an out-of-date way of attention grabbing since it's such an obvious one, but it still goes on, though possibly is the province of the desperate.

Creating a Problem to Solve the Problem

One of the most difficult bullshit activities to spot, but one of the most common. Typically the corporate bullshitter will call a meeting with the boss and team to discuss a problem that most of them didn't know existed. The team will be dispatched to "fix the problem." After a suitable time has elapsed and with no success by the team, the bullshitter will leap into action to solve the problem, neatly appearing to the boss as a savior and promotion candidate.

Employ Someone to Take the Heat, Then Fire Him for Failure or Take Credit for His Success

Typically the corporate bullshitter will have been given an important task; this person will then employ someone else to do the work, neatly ensuring that if it goes wrong there's someone fireable in place to take the blame. If it's a success, the fake can still present the work as his own.

Empire Building

A term used to describe people who expand their teams and take on bigger areas of responsibility in an attempt to appear indispensable. It's also a good ploy for getting a pay raise; the bigger the team, the more you should earn.

Featherbedding

This is an old term from the days when unions had such power they could pressure companies to employ more people than they actually needed to perform a specific task. The bullshitter uses the same technique to make it look as if their teams are bigger than they really are; therefore the manager is more important and deserves his big paycheck.

Finding Out the Boss's Interests

Is the boss a fan of country or hip-hop? Does he or she read Dickens or Dan Brown? The bullshitter will find out and spookily become a fan of the same.

Gadgetry

Providing the boss is technically savvy, being seen with the latest handheld device will look good. The right mobile phone is also essential; it must look good and have a ring tone that isn't tacky but shows some sophistication. Think more Björk than Britney.

Ignoring What's Right

A sure sign of a bullshitter and someone who is only looking after number 1, is when a situation arises where there is one obvious course of action for the good of the team. The fake will ignore it and do what is right for her and her career. It's about looking right, not being right.

Laughing Loudly at an Unfunny Joke Made by a Senior Manager

A sad activity, it just encourages them to make more bad jokes.

Praising the Boss

One of the oldest in the book, but it works.

Putting the Bullshitter's Name in the Footnotes of Presentations and Spreadsheets

A common trick; even if the culprits didn't do the work, it looks like they did.

Sex

Sexy people are the best bullshitters; all their victims think about is how gorgeous they are. All the while the bullshitters are undermining them with their short skirts, tight bums, and winning smiles . . . and that's just the men.

Summarizing the Boss's Ideas and Feeding It Back to Him or Her

Skilled bullshitters will listen to what the boss has to say, pull out the salient points, and replay it back to the boss using similar words. This gives the impression that they are on the same side as the boss and understand fully what he/she wants. Faking empathy is a great skill; it can appear insincere, but when it works it's very effective.

Swearing to Give Credibility
Using four-letter words to give a bit of cred was very much a male pastime, but now women engage in this too in an attempt to be "one of the boys" or to prove how tough they can be.

Taking the Lead During Presentations
"You're only as good as your last presentation" is a motto often touted by the most successful fakes. Have you ever noticed how the best presenters always get ahead?

Talking Loudly
One for open-plan offices, the technique is to wait for the boss to be around, then be heard talking on the phone using words and phrases like "the numbers," "deal," "contract," or "customer" while giving sideways glances to see that the boss is listening.

Walking Purposefully
The walk is very important; it is essential to look like an important mission is involved, one that is vital to the future of the company. Ideally you must carry a clipboard or piece of paper, though the real aficionados will be walking around with envelopes marked CONFIDENTIAL or TOP SECRET.

2. Leaders and Managers

Leadership is the art of getting someone else to do something you want done because he wants to do it.
—Dwight D. Eisenhower

Leadership

According to business guru Peter Drucker, the four key skills of a leader are as follows:

1. Listening
2. Communicating
3. Not using alibis
4. Realizing that the leader is less important than the task at hand

We have a fifth:

5. Bullshitting. Whether Drucker likes it or not, it's what's needed to get ahead in the real world

Remember these when next dealing with your boss.

The business guru and the media have created several types of leader and have dictated their recognizable traits. Here are our interpretations, plus a few that we've learned about along the way.

Articulate/Inadequate

Looks great, sounds great, and knows nothing.

Motto: Looking good!

Chameleon

Out for themselves and no one else, these bullshitters par-excellence will change views to whatever they feel is the prevailing one or the one that gives them the best advantage.

Motto: What's your view?

Conflict Avoider

Hates any sort of argument, doesn't really like people, and manages the team by e-mail to avoid contact.

Motto: Anything you like, really.

Deal Junkie

Just likes doing deals, no leadership skills whatsoever. Will turn everything into a negotiation.

Motto: Come on. Let's discuss this; we're in a partnership, here . . .

Easygoing, Nice

Not bothered about deadlines, will use terms like **"end of play"** instead of "I want it on my desk by four p.m." A manager to be taken advantage of. Never successful, too well liked, and not ruthless enough.

Motto: Sure, whatever . . .

Flatterer

Compliments, unctuousness, and general ability to brown-nose.

Motto: You look just fantastic . . .

Goal-oriented
> There's a target for everything. . . .
> *Motto: So what's next?*

Hard
> They're tough and overly competitive.
> *Motto: Take no prisoners.*

Impatient
> Always stressed, inefficient, always missing deadlines.
> *Motto: I need it yesterday.*

Indecisive
> Can't make their mind up, obsessive tinkering with plans
> and ideas.
> *Motto: Yes and no, maybe . . .*

Inspirational
> True leaders. When you're with them you feel great, but in-
> teractions usually have no substance beyond the obvious.
> They tell you only good things and forget you the mo-
> ment you leave their field of vision.
> *Motto: We can do it; together we're a great team. . . .*

Lazy
> Couldn't care less what happens, hoping to get fired with a
> good severance.
> *Motto: You're mistaking me for someone who gives a shit.*

Look-at-me
> Always the first to volunteer, takes credit for the work of the
> team, ruthless.
> *Motto: Me, me, me.*

Machiavellian
A political, cunning, deceitful little weasel.
Motto: One goal, my goal.

Mom or Dad, Family
Sees their team as their children, very protective, slightly embarrassing, and a little crazy.
Motto: We're in this together (said earnestly).

Mushroom
Keeps the team in the dark and feeds them shit.
Motto: Information is power.

Numbers
Can't do anything without a spreadsheet in front of them.
Motto: I ❤ Excel

Pervert
Wouldn't want to meet them in a dark alley.
Motto: No motto, just a pair of good binoculars and a little mirror stuck to the top of their shoe.

Power Crazed, Empire Builder
Always empire building, always in competition with everyone else.
Motto: The more people in my team, the more power I have. . . .

Psychopath, Sadist
Loves to watch their team suffer, just for fun, but is nice about it.
Motto: And how are you today?

Puppy Dog
Want to be liked, will agree to and say anything just to be popular, useless managers. This style leads to lots of arguments within their team.
Motto: That's a great idea. Well done.

Risk Averse
Won't make commitments in case it backfires on them; similar to the **Indecisive** but won't entertain new ideas at all.
Motto: We'll pass on it this time. . . .

Ruthless
Quiet, shows no mercy, and enjoys being a complete shit, not likeable, no personality.
Motto: No pain no gain.

Savvy
Always aware of what's going on, streetwise and a player.
Motto: Understand . . .

Schizoid
Says one thing, means another, and does something else.
Motto: They'll never know . . . or maybe they will . . .

Seagull
Flies overhead, makes a lot of noise, lands, shits on the team, and flies off when the going gets tough.
Motto: See you later . . .

Sensitive Soul
Cares deeply and manages the team by e-mail in case they say something nasty.
Motto: Are you OK? It's not me, is it?

Slide-rule
The analytical and intellectual approach to management.
Motto: According to my analysis . . .

Snooper
This person manages by personal intrusiveness, prying, and spying. It's called *snoopervison*.
Motto: Really, and what else did they say?

Stepford Manager
Looks great, sounds great, and agrees with everyone. Slightly robotic, perfect tan, can do no wrong in the boss's eyes.
Motto: I concur.

Strategy Man
Just sees the wider view, can't do detail.
Motto: OK, you can take it from here.

Stress Monkey
Always in a panic, everything is a nightmare, transmits stress to their team. A member of staff will eventually hit back.
Motto: Oh my God, it's a nightmare!

Teflon
Always fucking up but never gets the blame for their mistakes.
Motto: It was him . . .

The 404
From the Internet error message: mistake-prone and basically dumb.
Motto: Oh shit . . . oops.

Troubleshooter

So busy solving other people's problems, they don't do any actual managing of their own team.

Motto: You don't want to do it like that. Do it like this . . .

Wimp

Completely dominated by their team, unable to cope with leading.

Motto: You do it, please.

Workaholic

Does everyone's work for them, doesn't trust anyone enough to actually delegate.

Motto: I'll do it.

Inspiring and Managing the Troops

As a newcomer trying to make a mark, you often get advice from old sages, mentors, well-meaning colleagues, and of course bullshitters who are trying to set you up. Here are some of the classic words and phrases found in that advice.

Abandonment

MEANING: Leaving, letting go.

BULLSHIT: In other words, know what to take on and what to leave aside. A key management skill or the sign of a lazy git?

Align, Alignment

MEANING: Ally oneself, almost agree but not so that you can't backtrack later.

BULLSHIT: Useful, especially in confrontational situations. "Are we aligned on this?" allows people who don't wholly agree with the proposition to save face. In practice it means decisions are just postponed or hidden and actions are taken outside the public arena.

Bang the Drum

MEANING: Make a fuss, get publicity, promote.

BULLSHIT: In the world of the office, the bullshitter bangs his own drum, not the company's.

Benchmarking

MEANING: Comparing to specific or agreed standards, comparing the best practices used in other companies in order to improve performance.

BULLSHIT: A classic bullshit term as it can be used to demonstrate breadth of experience and ability to see the wider view. Used by consultants to extend their contracts. "We'll have to benchmark extensively so that we can get a holistic view of the market in all its guises. This work should take us, oh, a year."

Bootstrap

MEANING: To complete something successfully without outside help or by one's own efforts.

BULLSHIT: A nightmare for the company bullshitter because they can neither do it nor take credit for it when someone else does.

Carve Out a Niche

MEANING: Find a place where you will be valued, or a skill you will be known for.

BULLSHIT: It's good advice to become associated with something good, although too many newcomers are given their niche by more experienced managers who like to keep out of trouble. "Take this project," they will say. "It will be the making of you." Not.

Comfort Zone
MEANING: An environment or situation in which a person feels secure and comfortable as long as there is no drastic change. New managers are encouraged to get out of their comfort zones and take risks.

BULLSHIT: If all managers moved out of their comfort zones, think of the number of therapist jobs that would be created.

Convert Plans to Action
MEANING: Doing what you planned to do.

BULLSHIT: Many corporations go on about what plans they have without ever achieving any of them, though eventually it gets noticed. The great corporate PR trick is to get publicity by announcing some great plan to create new jobs without any intention of putting those plans in place.

Custodian
MEANING: Someone who owns or looks after an aspect of the business, see also **Stakeholder.**

BULLSHIT: Basically a self-important jerk.

Don't Rock the Boat; Don't Make Waves
MEANING: Don't make trouble.

BULLSHIT: Usually said to a difficult member of a team by their manager. Probably a good thing if all you want is to get yourself to middle management and stay there.

Easy, Tiger

MEANING: Calm down; don't rush in.

BULLSHIT: The company bullshitter will be suspicious of enthusiastic, hard-working people; they have the potential to show him up, do a good job, and get results. This has to be stopped, and "Easy, Tiger" will be used in a comradely way to calm the good worker down and restore order to the bullshitter's life. Also listen for **"You can't boil the ocean all at once."**

Eyes and Ears

MEANING: Observant, prying—a spy.

BULLSHIT: You know you're in trouble when your manager says, "I want you to be my eyes and ears on this one." Someone is being set up.

Fast Track

MEANING: To push something or someone through a process faster than usual, the fastest route to a goal.

BULLSHIT: In reality, everything and everyone is attempting to fast track, which means nothing actually gets done faster.

Final Piece of the Jigsaw

MEANING: Last piece in place, part of a bigger plan.

BULLSHIT: If you are described as the last piece of the jigsaw, watch out—most companies work on a last in, first out principle.

Food Chain

MEANING: A competitive hierarchy. Derived from the biological system where the weak are preyed upon by the strong. **Survival of the fittest** is also often heard in this context.

BULLSHIT: Getting to the top of the corporate food chain is the goal of most company bullshitters, or at the very least, being the biggest fish in their little pond.

Go the Extra Mile, Sweat Harder

MEANING: Do more than is expected.

BULLSHIT: "If you go the extra mile, you'll be noticed and get ahead." In other words, you'll do more work and the bullshit manager will get the credit.

Grasp the Nettle

MEANING: Take the opportunity without fear, even though it may hurt a bit.

BULLSHIT: It will hurt a lot, actually.

Gravitas

MEANING: Substance, weight, standing, dignity, and respect.

BULLSHIT: Developing gravitas is very desirable among leaders, although it can look like they're just **acting important**.

Grown-up

MEANING: Adult, mature.

BULLSHIT: Along with **acting important** and showing **gravitas**, it's important to appear to take things seriously. Being childish or funny is seen as immature and not a good career move, no matter how tempting it is. Ha!

Halo Effect

MEANING: One great achievement, trait, or benefit that gives a favorable view of the whole.

BULLSHIT: Often those good at presentations get promoted because of the halo effect, the logic being that if they are good at presentations it therefore means they're good at everything else, too. Then reality bites and everyone realizes that they were just good at presentations.

Hidden Agenda
MEANING: An undisclosed plan, usually with an ulterior motive.
BULLSHIT: The hidden agenda is integral to the human condition.

Hit the Ground Running
MEANING: Start fast, know what you're doing without training.
BULLSHIT: Managers like people who can do this; it saves time and energy on training and leaves them to do other things, like suck up to their own boss, for example.

In the Boss's Boat/Canoe
MEANING: One of the chosen few, a sign of possible promotion.
BULLSHIT: Generally a good sign, you're on their team and you are one of the chosen few. Of course if things go wrong and the boss gets fired, you get the push with them.

Incentives, Fruits of Success
MEANING: Rewards, bonuses, and the promise of promotion.
BULLSHIT: Funny how often it's mentioned. Usually eventually there's some reason for the bonus not to be paid or that promotion not to happen, only for the next carrot to be dangled . . . and the cycle repeats itself.

Influencer
MEANING: A person who has the ability to influence others successfully.

BULLSHIT: Companies love and hate influencers in equal measures. They know they need them, but don't trust them.

It's a Jungle Out There
MEANING: A visual allegory for a place characterized by intense and ruthless competition or the struggle for survival.

BULLSHIT: Watch your step; in some corporations it's true!

Knowledge, Know-how
MEANING: Acquiring experience, expertise, and skills, the **knowledge base** and the **knowledge worker** are common terms.

BULLSHIT: Knowledge is a powerful thing. Protect knowledge and use it wisely. The greater the knowledge acquired, the better the bullshit.

Levels of Honesty
MEANING: Don't tell lies but don't always give out the entire truth; be selective about what information is given.

BULLSHIT: Don't be honest; it doesn't pay. Rule number 1 in the bullshitter's manual.

A Lick and a Promise
MEANING: A superficial attempt.

BULLSHIT: Many company bullshitters are superficial, applying as little work as they can get away with, with the promise that they will do a better job at a later stage. In fact, whole careers have been built on this premise.

Lifeblood

MEANING: A vital part (of a business), e.g., staff.

BULLSHIT: An essential term in the use of flattery to any employee or team. Listen for **salt of the earth**, too.

Long Haul

MEANING: In for a long period of time, committed.

BULLSHIT: These days few people are in it for the long haul although many pretend they are, and are able to build good financial packages on that basis.

Managing Upward

MEANING: To control one's manager.

BULLSHIT: A key skill for any upwardly mobile purveyor of bullshit.

"No" Is Not in My Vocabulary

MEANING: Always positive, always finding a way to solve a problem, not accepting defeat.

BULLSHIT: To any manager who says this ask, "So you *are* a butt-kissing little fucker, then?"

No Pressure

MEANING: Easygoing, stress-free.

BULLSHIT: "No pressure," they will say, but either they're setting you up to fail or they don't give a shit.

On a Roll

MEANING: Sustained success.

BULLSHIT: The time when companies start to convince themselves of their genius. Generally a good time to get out.

On the Map
MEANING: Make a name for yourself.
BULLSHIT: Get known for something—anything—even if it's someone else's work.

Outcome- or Results-Driven
MEANING: Toward a specific outcome. By implication, this is a done with high levels of concentration.
BULLSHIT: To become an insensitive, single-minded shit.

Power Lunch, Working Breakfast
MEANING: Working over a meal.
BULLSHIT: It's been a while since Gordon Gekko declared that "lunch is for wimps," but many managers and workers work through lunchtimes and other meal times too. Feel for them, for they do not know that they will get no thanks in the end.

Prioritize
MEANING: Find precedence for tasks, usually established by order of importance or urgency.
BULLSHIT: What is the correct order of importance: making money for the company, profit, looking good, or keeping the boss happy? You decide.

Proactive
MEANING: Anticipating and acting with forethought instead of waiting for something to happen.
BULLSHIT: Bullshitters are rarely proactive, unless it's in their own self-interest to be so.

Profile

MEANING: Exposure, renown in the business, reputation, visibility.

BULLSHIT: For any company bullshitter, profile is extremely important. Concerned managers and mentors will advise young colleagues to do anything to get noticed. Usually this doesn't involve working hard or getting results; just making a good presentation to the senior managers is generally enough.

Retaliation, Getting It in First

MEANING: Get your own back, get revenge.

BULLSHIT: Paranoia rules in your corporation? Get your coat and go.

Robust

MEANING: Strong, with stamina.

BULLSHIT: Plans must be robust . . . staff must be robust . . . successful bullshit must be robust too.

Sink or Swim

MEANING: To fail or succeed without any alternatives.

BULLSHIT: In other words, we don't give a shit how you get on; we can find a replacement anytime and we can't be bothered to train you.

Squeaky Clean

MEANING: Untarnished, almost too clean.

BULLSHIT: To be cynical about people who have this image is probably about right, but some try to achieve an astonishingly high level of cleanliness nonetheless. If it's too good to be true, don't trust it.

Strong Work Ethic
MEANING: Compulsion to be a hard worker.
BULLSHIT: They're gonna love you . . . sucker.

Straight Answer
MEANING: The honest truth without gloss.
BULLSHIT: People avoid giving a straight answer because invariably it gets them into trouble or it hurts someone they like; it's as simple as that. In a recent survey in the United States, it was found that 90 percent of Americans lied regularly.

Tasking
MEANING: Assigning specific tasks.
BULLSHIT: Managers who **task** their team with **deliverables** and **goals** generally need locking up.

Tenacious
MEANING: Holding fast, not giving up easily.
BULLSHIT: A good quality, but most people are thinking, "oh, for God's sake, give it a rest."

Time Management
MEANING: The art of making the best use of time.
BULLSHIT: Generally a case of do as I say and not as I do, most senior managers have an assistant to manage their time, go shopping, pick the kids up from school, babysit, and so on.

Will to Win
MEANING: Competitive, strong, doesn't like losing.
BULLSHIT: Managers love their teams to develop a strong competitive streak as long as it's not aimed at them.

While most corporate bullshitters are highly competitive, they are able to disguise their will to win effectively. But don't be fooled; they're out to get you all the same.

Work/Life Balance
MEANING: The harmony between working and home life.

BULLSHIT: You'll be expected to work long hours and give up holidays and weekends; the trick is to look like you put in the time. Study your boss's working habits; be there at the same times. This only works if your boss is lazy; if he's a workaholic, you're doomed.

Work Smarter
MEANING: To give more thought to your work and to use your intelligence more proactively.

BULLSHIT: Will anyone explain what exactly working smarter means in practice? No, I thought not.

You Can Do It If You Believe You Can
MEANING: An attempt to build confidence in a team member who has a difficult task.

BULLSHIT: It should be followed by "because I can't be arsed."

You Scratch My Back and I'll Scratch Yours, aka Quid Pro Quo
MEANING: You do me a favor and I'll do you one.

BULLSHIT: Don't do it!!

Managing the Team
So it's time to talk to the team. Senior management wants you to get them on their side . . . to get **back on track, into the game, off the sidelines and onto the field** and so on . . .

What clichés and phrases will you use? Take your pick of these, but watch out: management has heard them before, even used a few.

Cocks on the Block
MEANING: If it goes wrong, we're all getting the ax.
BULLSHIT: Particularly unappealing to men, usually said with a slight wince and sounds particularly good if said with an upper-class English accent.

Consensual Bollocks
MEANING: You don't have to agree, just do as I say . . . I haven't time to mess about discussing things.
BULLSHIT: A term used by strong leaders who can't stand to debate or have an inability to work in a collegial way. So, that's nearly all of them then.

Dance Round the Handbags
MEANING: Prevaricate, put off making a decision; "stop dancing round your handbags and get on with it." Borrowed from the dance floor habit of piling up the handbags in the center of the group of women.
BULLSHIT: The favorite of impatient managers everywhere.

Disseminate
MEANING: Spread.
BULLSHIT: In the business world, people don't "relate" or "give out" information, they disseminate it; it sounds much more important.

Dovetail

MEANING: From a particular carpentry joint, to join together perfectly.

BULLSHIT: Often an illusion, as the joints are nearly always creaky.

Do You Read Me?

MEANING: Do you understand?

BULLSHIT: A favorite of aggressive senior managers who think that their staff is illiterate, doesn't listen, or just doesn't understand when they offer a simple instruction. Use of this phrase usually only shows their own stupidity.

Ducks in a Row

MEANING: Present a united front, be well organized and equally informed. Well prepared.

BULLSHIT: A classic, associated with ass-covering, and generally said in a way that blame is diverted away from the user.

Get Our Act Together

MEANING: Stop making mistakes and get it right.

BULLSHIT: A sure sign of desperation if this gets used, either that or the manager is a bit of a softie and it's the first stage toward an eventual bollocking.

Heads-up

MEANING: A warning.

BULLSHIT: "We must give a heads-up to the team." Meaning, something is going wrong and I want them to get me out of the deep shit I'm already in.

Holding Our Nerve

MEANING: Not panicking into taking unnecessary actions.

BULLSHIT: Difficult to achieve, as the natural reaction to any problem is to try to solve it—unless you're a lazy git, then holding your nerve should come naturally.

Jump Through Hoops

MEANING: To go to great efforts, derived from circus animals doing tricks.

BULLSHIT: Another cliché used to encourage the team to do more, although it's usually said "I'm not asking you to jump though hoops." But that's exactly what is expected.

Keep It Simple

MEANING: "Do the basics well and you'll get results . . ."

BULLSHIT: "Because you're too stupid to do anything more complicated."

Ramp It Up, Ratchet It Up, Pump Up the Volume, Pull Out All the Stops

MEANING: To increase, do significantly better, with immediate effect.

BULLSHIT: A range of phrases and exhortations bordering on pleas, often said as part of last-minute panic as a deadline looms.

Riding the Razor's Edge

MEANING: Close to failure, with disastrous results if it all goes wrong.

BULLSHIT: One of those phrases, like **cocks on the block** or **going tits up**, that brings a tear to the eye when you think about it too much.

Seamless

MEANING: Without breaks, efficient.

BULLSHIT: No breaks, effective communication, a vision of harmony and the impression that all is well—that's bullshit for you.

Stoke Up the Boiler, Boiler Room

MEANING: The boiler room is the so-called hub of any business, where decisions are made and the real work is done. Stoking it up is encouraging the workers to work harder.

BULLSHIT: The suckers.

There's No "I" in "Team"

MEANING: There's no place for individual agendas, which may get in the way of the team's ability to reach a target.

BULLSHIT: But the bullshitter will be thinking "there may not be an 'I' in 'team,' but there's a 'me' . . ."

Think Outside the Box/Think Outside the Square

MEANING: Think laterally; solve a problem by taking a different approach to the norm.

BULLSHIT: These sayings come into play when managers run out of ideas. By encouraging their team to think differently, they hope that something positive will happen. Most of the team meanwhile will be thinking "What box?"

Wake Up and Smell the Coffee

MEANING: An exhortation to become aware of something big that's happening.

BULLSHIT: Usually used when a manager desperately wants to rouse their team from some form of lethargy. Used too often, though, and the team just pokes fun at the user.

We're Going Tits Out on This One . . .
MEANING: Going all out, without holding anything back.
BULLSHIT: Women in the team just love this . . .

When the Going Gets Tough, the Tough Get Going
MEANING: The strong always rise to the challenge.
BULLSHIT: One for those managers inspired by military leaders, to be said when the team is under pressure, usually with a clenched fist punching the invisible foe. Try not to laugh.

Word on the Street
MEANING: What's going on, the latest news, gossip.
BULLSHIT: Any good manager will know what's going on; any good bullshitter will be creating the "word."

You Don't Have to Be Crazy to Work Here, but It Helps
MEANING: An old office sign not seen much these days, implying that the working environment is wacky and fun.
BULLSHIT: If you see this sign in an office, you know that it won't be wacky or fun, just full of sad individuals convincing themselves it's a great place to work. Get your coat and go.

You Guys
MEANING: You people.
BULLSHIT: Said when the speaker wants to appear nonconfrontational and inclusive . . . watch out!

BULLSHIT BINGO—Managers' Styles

ARTICULATE/ INADEQUATE	DEAL JUNKIE	CHAMELEON	CONFLICT AVOIDER	NUMBERS	LOOK-AT-ME	EASYGOING, NICE	EMPIRE BUILDER
SAVVY	SEAGULL	SLIDE-RULE	STRESS MONKEY	STRATEGY MAN	INFLUENCER	MOM OR DAD	WORKAHOLIC
FLATTERER	MUSHROOM	INDECISIVE	INSPIRATIONAL	HARD	IMPATIENT	PERVERT	SENSITIVE
POWER CRAZED	TROUBLE SHOOTER	PSYCHO-PATH/SADIST	LAZY	CUSTODIAN	GOAL-ORIENTED	THE 404 (ERROR-PRONE)	MACHIAVEL-LIAN
SCHIZOID	PUPPY DOG	TEFLON	STEP-FORD	RUTHLESS	WIMP	SNOOPER	RISK AVERSE

How to play: How many can you identify in your office?
See page 8 for interpretations.

BULLSHIT BINGO—The Team Talk

EYES AND EARS	FAST TRACK	SWEAT HARDER	GO THE EXTRA MILE	GRAVITAS
LONG HAUL	EASY, TIGER	GRASP THE NETTLE	HALO EFFECT	YOU GUYS
HOLDING OUR NERVE	JUMP THROUGH HOOPS	GROWN-UP	CONVERTING PLANS INTO ACTION	ROBUST
HIT THE GROUND RUNNING	RIDING THE RAZOR EDGE	PUMP UP THE VOLUME	INCENTIVE	GOING TITS OUT
NO PRESSURE	ALIGN	LIFEBLOOD	RAMP IT UP	PRIORITIZE
IT'S A JUNGLE OUT THERE	GET OUR ACT TOGETHER	COMFORT ZONE	DANCE ROUND YOUR HANDBAGS	PROSPEC-TIVE
KNOW HOW	ON THE MAP	COCKS ON THE BLOCK	BOILER ROOM	PROFILE
LICK AND A PROMISE	WHEN THE GOING GETS TOUGH . . .	OUTCOME	CUSTODIAN	BENCH-MARK
BANG THE DRUM	ON A ROLL	RESULTS-DRIVEN	GET OUR DUCKS IN A ROW	DISSEMI-NATE

How to play: Simply check off 6 words or phrases in one meeting and shout out BINGO!

3. War, Battles, Fighting, and Guns

Ah, this is obviously some strange usage of the word "safe" that I wasn't previously aware of.

—Arthur Dent
Hitchhiker's Guide to the Galaxy
by Douglas Adams

Here is where the fighting style of management takes over. It has to be said that this relatively unsophisticated and robust language is mainly used by men; women tend to use cleverer imagery, sometimes even likening themselves to characters such as Atlanta the Huntress and, surprisingly often, she-wolves.

Combative managers love taking center stage when there's a problem to be sorted out or a competitor to be taken on, turning a simple marketing plan into a major **field of operations** with **combatants** and an **enemy**. They love to imagine the smell of napalm or cordite filling the air. In reality though, it is actually the smell of bullshit.

A Bridge Too Far
    MEANING: From the title of the book by Cornelius Ryan and later the film by Richard Attenborough where the battle for the bridge at Arnhem proved too much for Allied troops.
    BULLSHIT: In this context it's applied to companies taking too big a chance. Using this phrase is risky, as you could seem negative. Not a good bullshit term.

Battleground

MEANING: Usually referring to the market in which the company is trading.

BULLSHIT: The place of work; **war zone** is the same as battleground, but it sounds more modern.

Battle Royal

MEANING: Probably originally from cockfighting, though more closely associated with ultraviolent Japanese films, it means an unusually fierce fight where the contestants have no choice but to engage.

BULLSHIT: Great for those on the outside looking in, not much fun for those involved.

Bite the Bullet

MEANING: Something has to be done, and it's painful. Derived from the fact that before anaesthetics, soldiers bit on a bullet to help cope with the pain.

BULLSHIT: A rare thing for a bullshitter to endure; usually there's a fall guy somewhere.

Bomb, Bombed

MEANING: To fail.

BULLSHIT: Usually used in a sales context and the bullshitter will have disappeared or found some poor loser to act as scapegoat. In the UK this sometimes means the opposite, which is confusing for them, especially when they're trying to bullshit Americans.

Fall on Your Sword

MEANING: To take the blame and lose your job in the process . . .

BULLSHIT: Usually with a nice severance package.

Going Great Guns
MEANING: Going exceptionally well. Apparently this stems from a British naval expression from the 1700s when "blowing great guns" meant a violent gale.
BULLSHIT: A lot of hot air.

Going Nuclear
MEANING: Getting out of hand in a big way.
BULLSHIT: As long as he or she is not involved, the company bullshitter will be happy.

Grenades
MEANING: Unexpected and unforeseen events.
BULLSHIT: The practiced bullshitter will always keep a few handy, just in case.

Hit Them Where It Hurts
MEANING: A competition-busting tactic to really do damage to another company.
BULLSHIT: Ouch!

In the Armory/Arsenal
MEANING: As in, "Have we got anything left in the arsenal?" Last tactics or new tricks to employ.
BULLSHIT: Usually the answer is no.

In the Trenches
MEANING: This is a bit like battleground, but involves the troops rather than senior management. The implication is that it's a much harder and longer affair.
BULLSHIT: Time to leave and find another company.

It's a War Out There
MEANING: It's a hostile environment.

BULLSHIT: A great saying for creating impact, but when it's about something like the toy or the lingerie market . . . well it's just not a war is it? You're taking it too seriously; see a therapist.

Kamikaze
MEANING: To do something suicidal, though not literally—just career-wise.

BULLSHIT: Something the bullshitter usually likes to watch a colleague or a competitor do. See also **Self-toaster** on page 122.

Keeping Your Powder Dry
MEANING: Originally referring to gunpowder, now used primarily with respect to keeping something back or not reacting to an initial attack.

BULLSHIT: Everyone holds something back except the honest, stupid, and naïve.

Lead from the Front, Leading the Line
MEANING: To take the initiative, be the first, show strong leadership qualities.

BULLSHIT: Those in front always take the first bullets and are first to tread on the land mines.

Live by the Sword, Die by the Sword
MEANING: If you live your life aggressively, then there's a high probability that it will end in the same way.

BULLSHIT: People who act in this way are always amazed when someone stabs them, especially as it's usually in the back.

Lock and Load
MEANING: Get ready for action.

BULLSHIT: Popularized in everything from John Wayne westerns to *Star Trek*, it should actually be load and lock, but there's Hollywood for you.

Lock, Stock, and Barrel
MEANING: The whole thing.

BULLSHIT: Originally from all the parts in a flintlock, now more associated with London gangsters so now people think they sound cool and hard-nosed by saying it. Sad.

Loose Cannon
MEANING: Someone who is unpredictable.

BULLSHIT: There's nothing more unsettling for senior management than when someone equally senior is saying something harmful about the company, albeit with the best intentions. It's great to watch, though.

Minefield
MEANING: Something littered with problems.

BULLSHIT: **Tap dancing in a minefield** is a descriptive way of saying "doing something risky while avoiding problems along the way."

Mines, Land Mines
MEANING: Problems.

BULLSHIT: Another image to conjure up here, managers will look at their plans, talk about how to access the **low-hanging fruit**, the **long-term goals**, the **short-term gains** and then ask if there are any likely land mines on the way. Bullshitters love laying them; the nightmare is finding them.

Mission Critical
MEANING: Vital to the success of the mission.
BULLSHIT: The main problem is that *everything* becomes mission critical.

Molotov Cocktails
MEANING: More problems, but ones to be created for the opposition.
BULLSHIT: A weapon beloved by the company bullshitter.

Preemptive Strike
MEANING: To attack first in anticipation of an attack from the opposition.
BULLSHIT: Not the usual bullshit tactic, as it could eventually lead to potential exposure and possible defeat. One for the gung-ho managers.

Shotgun Approach
MEANING: Take many different approaches toward the same goal.
BULLSHIT: Chuck enough shit at a wall, and some of it will stick.

Take the Flak
MEANING: Taking the blame or criticism . . .
BULLSHIT: Usually on behalf of someone who has set you up.

Wagons in a Circle
MEANING: From the practice of European settlers under attack from American Indians of putting their wagons in a circle to defend themselves.
BULLSHIT: Most people under thirty have no clue what this

means, never having seen a John Wayne movie. That won't stop older managers from using it though.

Waiting for the Cavalry to Arrive

MEANING: Waiting to be saved.

BULLSHIT: Another Hollywood-derived war term, many companies also have their **wagons in a circle** and are being **surrounded by bad guys**; it's a shame these sayings are going out of use, really.

Walking Wounded

MEANING: Those left after a battle, bloodied but able to move.

BULLSHIT: The poor saps who have to pick up the pieces.

Weapons-Grade

MEANING: Extra-strength, extreme.

BULLSHIT: As in, "you have a weapons-grade case there." Can't help thinking that this should be followed by "Big Boy!"

BULLSHIT BINGO—War

BATTLE-GROUND	GOING GREAT GUNS	IN THE ARSENAL	LEADING THE LINE	LOOSE CANNON	WAGONS IN A CIRCLE
A BRIDGE TOO FAR	BITE THE BULLET	IT'S A WAR OUT THERE	TAKE THE FLAK	LOCK, STOCK, AND BARREL	HIT THEM WHERE IT HURTS
MOLOTOV COCKTAILS	FALL ON YOUR SWORD	KEEP YOUR POWDER DRY	SHOTGUN APPROACH	LOCK AND LOAD	GOING NUCLEAR
TIPTOEING THROUGH THE MINEFIELD	SAVED BY THE CAVALRY	WALKING WOUNDED	MISSION CRITICAL	LIVE BY THE SWORD AND DIE BY THE SWORD	MINES
LAND MINES	IN THE ARMORY	BOMBED	PREEMPTIVE STRIKE	KAMIKAZE	WEAPONS-GRADE
MINEFIELD	LEAD FROM THE FRONT	GRENADES	BOMB	ON THE CHARGE	IN THE TRENCHES

How to play: Simply check off 6 words in one meeting and shout out BINGO!

4. Excuses, Disasters, and Why It All Went Wrong

No one is interested, until you make a mistake . . .
—Anonymous

In Big Business it's mainly a matter of luck as to whether things work out well, especially in public companies where the overwhelming need to offer something positive to shareholders every year prevents real long-term planning.

Covering his or her back, setting up scapegoats, and having credible excuses in hand is a major part of the company bullshitter's job, and for some it really is an art form. For outsiders it's a complete mystery, but it's all about doing everything possible to keep their jobs.

Here's a few of the most common terms and excuses. Get the violin ready . . .

20-20 Hindsight
MEANING: Looking back with perfect clarity.
BULLSHIT: Reviewing mistakes that with 20-20 hindsight simply look very obvious.

A Rising Tide That Lifts All Boats
MEANING: We're all in this together.
BULLSHIT: Usually said by a senior executive when referring

to a company-wide issue, the real meaning being that they're in the shit and everyone is going down with them. Often followed up with "when the tide goes out, all the wrecks are visible," as the boss is looking for someone to blame. Interesting that some sources indicate that JFK used this expression to the effect that everyone benefited, but we like our version.

Asking the Impossible
MEANING: A request to do an unlikely task or achieve an unattainable goal.

BULLSHIT: Some managers will say, "I'm not asking the impossible" while knowing they are. They think they'll get better results, but their staff just lose heart.

Ass-Saving Exercise
MEANING: An attempt to save oneself.

BULLSHIT: Beloved by managers everywhere, the ass-saving exercise is standard practice for all those who want to apportion blame elsewhere.

At the End of the Day
MEANING: In the end.

BULLSHIT: Usually said in the context of "at the end of the day we have to bloody well do something . . ." The last few words are said in a high-pitched voice.

Ball-Juggling
MEANING: Coping with several tasks at once.

BULLSHIT: A common habit, sometimes referring to the art of juggling tasks, but also used in reference to inexperienced or nervous male managers who, as they present their latest plan, try to look relaxed by putting a hand in their pocket. The extent of their nervousness or even level of concentration is given away by how much they play with their testicles.

Balls in the Air

MEANING: To cope with several tasks at once, akin to a juggler with several balls in the air.

BULLSHIT: Some will tell you that management is all about keeping as many balls in the air as possible, but it's also about keeping spinning plates spinning and any other multitasking imagery you care to name. It's used by those who just want to appear busy, but beware of managers who talk constantly about how big their team is and how much their turnover is, just to impress. With more than six **direct reports**, they are either exceptional or their boss is setting them up to fail.

Between a Rock and a Hard Place

MEANING: Caught between two unpalatable solutions.

BULLSHIT: Staff members are asked do something that they know is fundamentally wrong but lack the courage to tell the boss why. They know that if they do as asked and it goes wrong (and they know it will) they'll get the blame but are helpless to prevent it.

Big Ask

MEANING: A large request, huge favor, or a difficult target.

BULLSHIT: "It's a big ask," says your colleague while appearing to suck a lemon. A common tactic in budget negotiations, usually the sign of a desperate effort to reduce targets. Watch the body language for collar tugging and chair shifting, and you should get an idea of how desperate they really are.

Blamestorm
MEANING: A period after something has gone wrong when blame is being apportioned.

BULLSHIT: Time to watch your back, as managers will be trawling the office to find someone else to blame for their shortcomings and failures.

Bloodbath
MEANING: A massacre, a period when there are lots of sackings.

BULLSHIT: The theory is that by announcing the sackings all at once, all the publicity happens in one shot. It may also hide many other issues that the company doesn't want to advertise.

Catch-22
MEANING: From Joseph Heller's outstanding novel, the original Catch-22 was the premise that anyone who applied to get out of U.S. military service on the grounds of insanity was behaving rationally and thus couldn't be insane.

BULLSHIT: It's (usually erroneously) used to describe any number of situations where it seems there's no way out.

Compliance
MEANING: Agreeing to a request, doing what's been asked.

BULLSHIT: A common worry for companies that depend on other companies to sell their products. For example, a manufacturer may buy space in a supermarket chain to promote the latest wonder product, only to find that many stores in the chain don't put the product out on display. This is poor compliance on behalf of the supermarket chain. It's a great excuse if sales look poor; just get a few photos of crappy displays to back the case.

Deep Diving
MEANING: Detailed analysis combined with problem-solving.
BULLSHIT: A great bullshitting term used to describe a very detailed investigation of a business, project, or situation. "It's gone wrong; we must do some *deep diving* to find out why." People will think you're extra clever for using this one.

Disappear Up Your Own Back Side/Behind
MEANING: Get so complicated and too convoluted to understand.
BULLSHIT: When attempting to solve a convoluted problem you can apparently actually physically disappear up your own ass in an attempt to get an answer.

Enough on My Plate
MEANING: Too much to do (so they say).
BULLSHIT: Yeah right, lazy jerk.

Fence Mending
MEANING: Repairing relationships.
BULLSHIT: For some reason this always gets applied to political relationships between countries, but most managers spent their time **mending fences, building bridges,** and **knocking down barriers.**

Fluid
MEANING: Unclear, unresolved.
BULLSHIT: One of the great delaying words, the situation is always *fluid.* Anything can happen; best to wait until we're sure . . . and so on.

From Day One
MEANING: From the start.
BULLSHIT: "It never worked from day one, but we kept going anyway."

Genie Is out of the Bottle
MEANING: To let something bad or unwanted happen, which cannot then be stopped.
BULLSHIT: A nightmare for the company bullshitter; they will go into overdrive attempting to apportion blame elsewhere and minimize their exposure.

Get Back to Basics
MEANING: Going back to fundamental practices, nothing fancy.
BULLSHIT: A classic, often used when a corporation has gone through a bad patch and got away from what they are good at. Usually heard when new management has arrived and feels the need to sort things out. When this is bandied about, it's probably right to leave, or of course you could come up with a great solution to save the company.

In the Pipeline
MEANING: Being planned, on its way.
BULLSHIT: One of the great excuse phrases; when the work hasn't been done, it's *in the pipeline*.

Kick in the Ass
MEANING: A severe telling-off geared to motivate a team.
BULLSHIT: It's usually done just for effect, so well into the realms of corporate bullshit.

Last-Chance Saloon
MEANING: Out of options, near the end.
BULLSHIT: A favorite of journalists, defeatist managers, and realists.

Left Hand Not Knowing What the Right Hand Is Doing
MEANING: Lack of communication, people acting in a certain way assuming that colleagues are doing the same.
BULLSHIT: A classic and a very common occurrence in businesses everywhere.

Less Is More
MEANING: Make more by doing less.
BULLSHIT: A true bullshit classic, this is a mantra often repeated by executives who work in a complex business and who don't understand it.

Limited Bandwidth
MEANING: Lack of resources.
BULLSHIT: When applied to people it can mean they are too busy or usually by implication that they are just thick.

Lose the Plot
MEANING: Get badly distracted from the main cause or issue.
BULLSHIT: When companies lose the plot, it means they're close to **meltdown**, shares are in **free fall**, and they're a **basket case**. When people lose the plot in the office, they're classed as nuts and entertaining in equal measures.

Naming and Shaming
MEANING: Highlighting and embarrassing those who have committed an offense or made a mistake.

BULLSHIT: Something the company bullshitter takes great delight in, provided s/he is not involved.

Nest-guarding
MEANING: Keeping information in an attempt to maintain a position of power or justify a role.

BULLSHIT: Less overt than **empire building**, most managers do this when they feel under threat, which in some companies is most of the time and a major reason why they're not doing well.

Nightmare
MEANING: A horrifying experience.

BULLSHIT: The stressed and the panicked love this word. They flounce round the office saying, "oh my god, it's a nightmare!" when usually they've just run out of paper clips.

No-Win Situation
MEANING: Whatever happens, you can't win.

BULLSHIT: One of the great excuses for the bullshitting manager; usually there's a way out of any situation but it would mean losing face or doing something radical, which means taking a risk and possible exposure.

Noise on the Line
MEANING: Distractions.

BULLSHIT: Author: "I've got so much noise on the line, I can't finish this book on time." Publisher: "Just fucking finish it, or my boys will pay a visit."

Non-core

MEANING: Nonessential, not central to the issue.

BULLSHIT: The first departments to go in a company re-structure are always those where either the manager hasn't fought sufficiently hard for their cause or those that are considered non-core by whoever is responsible for **reengineering** the business—usually anything creative.

Ohnosecond

MEANING: The second that you realize something went horribly wrong.

BULLSHIT: A company bullshitter's nightmare.

Open-Heart Surgery

MEANING: Major repairs.

BULLSHIT: A company needing open-heart surgery is in real trouble. Of course, new management taking over the stricken beast will always want others to believe the problem's worse than it really is so that when recovery happens it looks all the better.

Out of the Loop

MEANING: Not included.

BULLSHIT: "I was out of the loop on this one." A great "not me" excuse if ever there was one.

Park It

MEANING: Put to one side to be dealt with later.

BULLSHIT: The province of managers who only want to discuss items on their own agenda and nothing else. The parked items are rarely returned to.

Quick Fix

MEANING: A running repair, short-term repair.

BULLSHIT: The quick fix is very common, particularly in those companies listed on the stock exchange that have to justify their actions once a year. It's a symptom of **short-term thinking** and an overwhelming desire to keep bad news from shareholders.

Read the Riot Act

MEANING: Give a serious telling-off, so named after the 1715 Riot Act in England where if a group of more than twelve people didn't disperse after the Riot Act was read to them, they could be legally arrested.

BULLSHIT: Good job it was repealed in 1986, now usually associated with empty threats.

Rearranging the Deck Chairs on the Titanic

MEANING: Pointlessly making changes in the face of an impending disaster.

BULLSHIT: Particularly apt for the period just before a corporation goes into a disastrous trading period, when the management desperately apply unworkable remedies in the hope that something will save them.

Risk Averse

MEANING: Hates taking risks, cowardly by implication, cautious by nature.

BULLSHIT: Frustrating to work with, as nothing really gets done without team members taking things into their own hands and taking risks on their manager's behalf.

Risk Factor
MEANING: Something that increases the risk or likelihood of something going wrong.

BULLSHIT: The risk-averse and cautious manager sees dangers everywhere. The company bullshitter will come up with a few that were previously not thought of just to wind them up.

Save Our Bacon
MEANING: Rescuing a situation.

BULLSHIT: Substitute the "our" in this phrase with "my," and you'll be nearer the truth.

Secondhand Bullshit
MEANING: Repetition of other people's bullshit.

BULLSHIT: A real crime for the company bullshitter and frustrating for everyone else.

Shambles
MEANING: A complicated mess.

BULLSHIT: In the company bullshitter's mind, a shambles is what happens when other people get it wrong. When it happens to them, it's a complex and variable situation.

Shit Hit the Fan
MEANING: A good visual metaphor meaning when something goes wrong, it will leave a right mess.

BULLSHIT: Whoever came up with this phrase deserves some sort of medal.

Shit or Get Off the Pot
MEANING: To do or die.

BULLSHIT: The province of the desperate and the unwise.

Shoot One's Self in the Foot
MEANING: Something that backfires or a mistake that comes back to haunt you.

BULLSHIT: *Schadenfreude* is a wonderful thing, although not if you're the one who made the mistake.

Skeletons in the Closet
MEANING: Unknown issues or hidden problems arising.

BULLSHIT: Well, we've all got our little secrets haven't we?

Sledgehammer to Crack a Nut
MEANING: An over-the-top solution to a small problem.

BULLSHIT: A common problem in businesses today, where an inordinate amount of time and money goes into solving small problems when larger issues get ignored. People make a show of problem-solving just to get noticed.

Stick to the Knitting
MEANING: Do the things you are good at; don't try to be too clever.

BULLSHIT: This is what most corporations should do, but they get overly ambitious or complacent and it all ends in tears.

Suboptimal
MEANING: Below standard.

BULLSHIT: In some areas of business these days it's just not right to say that something has been fucked up or performance is pitiful. No, it has to be *suboptimal*; it's much less confrontational.

Systemic
MEANING: Of a whole system or body.

BULLSHIT: "I think you'll find the problem is systemic," says the worker. "Systemic? It's got a fungal infection?" says the boss. Yes this actually happened . . . see also *The 404*.

Throw in Everything, Including the Kitchen Sink
MEANING: Hold nothing back.

BULLSHIT: A bit desperate, but common—in end-of-season sales for example.

Throw the Baby out with the Bathwater
MEANING: Destroying something good while ridding yourself of something bad.

BULLSHIT: Surprisingly common, especially when new management arrives and is keen to make their mark.

Tits Up
MEANING: Going wrong.

BULLSHIT: An enduring image in some circumstances.

TLC
MEANING: Tender Loving Care.

BULLSHIT: For when things are just a little bit wrong. Rather, completely fucked. Bless them.

Took a Haircut (Took a Bath) on That One
MEANING: Took a loss.

BULLSHIT: Apparently common parlance in some offices—weird or what?

Vacuum Up

MEANING: Clean up after the mess, take into account everything missed.

BULLSHIT: Usually the job of some poor sap who's been
brought in to sort out something that went wrong.

Where to from Here?

MEANING: What's the next action? . . .

BULLSHIT: . . . because I haven't a clue.

BULLSHIT BINGO—Excuses, and Why It All Went Wrong . . .

20-20 HINDSIGHT	NIGHTMARE	FROM DAY ONE	OPEN-HEART SURGERY	OUT OF THE LOOP	BALL-JUGGLING
NO-WIN SITUATION	ENOUGH ON MY PLATE	FLUID	LIMITED BAND-WIDTH	IN THE PIPELINE	BLAMESTORM
ASS-SAVING EXERCISE	BACK TO BASICS	DEEP DIVING	FENCE MENDING	DISAPPEAR UP YOUR OWN BEHIND	COMPLIANCE
A RISING TIDE THAT LIFTS ALL BOATS	BLOODBATH	LESS IS MORE	ASKING THE IMPOSSIBLE	QUICK FIX	SUBOPTIMAL
CATCH-22	BALLS IN THE AIR	AT THE END OF THE DAY . . .	BIG ASK	NON-CORE	SYSTEMIC
NOISE ON THE LINE	BETWEEN A ROCK AND A HARD PLACE	LEFT HAND NOT KNOWING WHAT THE RIGHT IS DOING	REARRANGING THE DECK CHAIRS ON THE *TITANIC*	RISK FACTOR	STICK TO THE KNITTING

How to play: Simply check off 6 words or phrases in one meeting and shout out BINGO!

5. Politics, PR, and Spin

The best minds are not in government. If any were, business would hire them away.

—Ronald Reagan

Politics is so rife with clichés, double meanings, and media bullshit alongside the political fakery that it warrants a whole book devoted to the subject. As we're mostly concerned with office bullshit, we'll content ourselves with a few relevant terms and a couple of bingo cards, one specially designed to get you through a political interview.

PR and spin are all about bullshit, the art of making something appear more positive than it really is, the covering up of wrongdoings, and passing the buck.

Sadly the real problems often get ignored because **spin doctors** and politicians are so busy covering their backsides and getting their message across that they can't see the most obvious solutions.

Here are a few areas of classic bullshit, clichés, and spin.

Bear with Me

MEANING: Stick with me because I want to say something I think is important . . .

BULLSHIT: . . . and I don't want to answer your question.

Became a Politician to Make a Difference in People's Lives
MEANING: A will to do good in the community.

BULLSHIT: A few hard-working politicians actually do try to do some good, but for the majority it's about power and bullshit.

Big Lie
MEANING: A whopper so large it must be true because no one would dare say it if it wasn't. A trick inherited from the Nazis and Dr. Joseph Goebbels who said, "If you tell a lie big enough and keep repeating it, people will eventually come to believe it."

BULLSHIT: Amazingly, people still actually try this one . . . and people still fall for it.

Bumping
MEANING: Taking something potentially damaging said in the media . . .

BULLSHIT: . . . and replacing it with something less damaging.

Categorical Denial
MEANING: A complete rebuttal of the accusation.

BULLSHIT: Generally if someone offers up a categorical denial, they're hoping that by being firm about it the problem will go away. Sadly for them, it usually doesn't.

Demonstrated Real Leadership
MEANING: Shown that they're not as weak as everyone thought.

BULLSHIT: This is usually done with the conniving help of a sympathetic media, until they get bored and support someone else.

Flip-flopping

MEANING: To announce something to the press only to retract or contradict it soon afterward.

BULLSHIT: A great way to cause confusion and take everyone's eye off the real agenda.

Focus on the Issues, Not Personalities

MEANING: Not insulting the opposition but concentrating on policies and what is actually going to get done.

BULLSHIT: Politicians always say they're going to do this but never do. It's always easier to be destructive than constructive and it gets better headlines.

Grass Roots

MEANING: Local, common people.

BULLSHIT: A patronizing term to describe what goes on at the level of politics where people do the real work. Sometimes they rise up and do something at a national level, like get rid of the leader.

Just Let Me Finish

MEANING: Usually said while being interrupted and when the politician wants to make a point, no matter what anyone else thinks.

BULLSHIT: Very common in American political talk and radio shows.

Laying the Foundation

MEANING: Starting something.

BULLSHIT: Politicians never start anything—they lay the foundation, **prepare the ground**, and generally imply that things are much more important than they really are.

Man of the People

MEANING: Has an understanding of what people are looking for from a leader, a good guy with working-class values and credentials. It's a term rarely applied to women.

BULLSHIT: A difficult thing to achieve, as it can be perceived as disingenuous or patronizing; most politicians are pretending to understand what the people want based on polls, the media, and market research.

Mandate

MEANING: Authority to do something.

BULLSHIT: These days often applied to the size of a government's majority; the bigger the majority, the bigger the mandate. It's not necessarily true that when a government gets in power with a strong mandate, they'll actually do what they said they would do in order to get that mandate.

Moral High Ground

MEANING: A position of strength dictated by the virtuous superiority of one person's position over another.

BULLSHIT: One of the key arts of bullshitting is to gain the moral high ground, especially when one has no right to be there.

Ordinary, Decent, Hardworking People

MEANING: The common man, normal people.

BULLSHIT: Often used by a senior government official to give the electorate the impression that s/he is on their side. This is not true, of course.

Our Children's Future Is at Stake

MEANING: By implication, storing up trouble for future generations.

BULLSHIT: Tugging at the heartstrings here. After all, who would want to hurt the poor little kiddies? Often said by opposition parties; watch out for U-turns once in power.

Polls and Statistics

MEANING: Politics, polls, and statistics go hand in hand with business, usually in very underhanded ways.

BULLSHIT: Essentially the trick is to quote figures that put the speaker's party in good light or trash the opposition's policies, then repeat the statistics (even if they're wrong or dubious) as often as possible. The same technique applies in business; it's amazing how fast something becomes the truth if it's repeated often enough.

Smoking Gun

MEANING: Indisputable evidence.

BULLSHIT: There's no smoking gun in the White House, the Pentagon, or the boss's office. It's somewhere else . . . honest.

Spin

MEANING: The process of putting something in a positive light.

BULLSHIT: So that's bullshit, then.

Teflon

MEANING: Nonstick chemical.

BULLSHIT: Whether Teflon politicians or managers, they never seem to get into trouble when something they are responsible for goes wrong. Ronald Reagan was nicknamed the Teflon President for this "skill."

We Have to Look to the Future
MEANING: Prepare, be prepared.

BULLSHIT: In other words, wait until we get into power, then we can change everything.

Will of the People
MEANING: What the electorate wants.

BULLSHIT: What we want the electorate to think they want.

With All Due Respect
MEANING: I'm sorry, but . . .

BULLSHIT: When people say "with all due respect," in fact they mean the opposite.

Wizard of Oz
MEANING: A 1939 Oscar-winning fantasy film.

BULLSHIT: When they run out of ideas, political commentators get desperate and start comparing politicians to Tin Men, Cowardly Lions, Wicked Witches, and Dorothy.

Bullshitters' Tips on How to Be a Successful Politician

1. Always dress smartly, unless it's good spin to be seen casually dressed, e.g., on the presidential ranch.
2. Never give a straight answer. If you have to, then make sure there are plenty of caveats and a get-out clause, or a scapegoat.
3. Believe your own lies; a lack of conscience always helps, as does an ability to pretend you care.
4. Never apologize, unless it puts you in a good light.
5. Be completely unembarrassed about maintaining double standards.
6. Be aware of the previous policies of your competition, they will be useful.

7. Extol Christian values and virtues but only if you're fairly virtuous. If not, then make sure you have a good lawyer.
8. Become religious but be mainstream, not extreme.
9. Ensure you get good media training. When interviewed, learn the art of deflection. When asked a question, reply in such a way that you put across the points that you want to talk about.
10. Never take responsibility for anything; be ambiguous.
11. Cultivate the ability to turn unpopular actions into heroic deeds.
12. Take advantage of every legal freebie you can.
13. If you are male, ensure that your wife (you must be married) is attractive but not so attractive that she takes attention away from you. Never become the golden couple.
14. If you are female, ensure that your husband is anonymous, particularly if you are attractive. Never become a golden couple.
15. Keep your children away from the media.
16. Never become too closely associated with a single cause unless you are happy to be sidelined.
17. Don't be too bland, slick, clever, unpleasant, irascible, old-fashioned, or trendy (especially if you're over forty).
18. Choose a car that isn't too flashy but not too sensible; ensure that the brand is right and not too foreign.
19. Be seen recycling.
20. Always have a fall-back position or at least a fall guy to take the blame.
21. If you don't think you can do any of the above, then just tell the truth and the hell with it.

Here instead of a political bingo card, we thought it a good idea to honor those things said and heard by political interviewers, who at least attempt to get some straight answers.

BULLSHIT BINGO—Political Interview

I ASK YOU AGAIN	BEAR WITH ME	GOOD QUESTION	WE WANT TO SEND A SIGNAL	DESPITE THE FACT THAT . . .	LET'S LOOK AT . . .
I'VE ALREADY ANSWERED THAT QUESTION	REAL LEADERSHIP	WELL I WOULD ANSWER, BUT YOU KEEP INTERRUPTING	YOU ARE ABSOLUTELY CON-FIDENT OF THAT, ARE YOU?	DO YOU ACCEPT ANY RESPONSIBILITY?	YOU HAVE ABSOLUTELY NO IDEA, HAVE YOU?
COME ON!	JUST ANSWER THE QUESTION	YOUR POINT IS WHAT?	CHANGING POLITI-CAL LANDSCAPE	THERE'S NO EXCUSE, IS THERE?	CAN WE JUST BE CLEAR.
WITH ALL DUE RESPECT	BUT YOU SAID . . .	YOU DON'T KNOW?	IS THAT PARTY POLICY?	HYPOTHETICALLY	YES OR NO?
PLEASE LET ME FINISH	REALLY?	DO YOU SUB-SCRIBE TO THAT VIEW?	SO THAT'S A NO, THEN?	GIVE US A FIGURE	IS THAT REAL OR JUST MADE UP?
THE POINT HERE IS . . .	ARE YOU BEING ENTIRELY FRANK?	SO, IN SUMMARY . . .	SO THAT'S A YES, IS IT?	DESPITE EVIDENCE TO THE CONTRARY	I'M GLAD YOU ASKED THAT . . .

How to play: Simply check off 6 words or phrases in one program and shout out BINGO!

6. Business Guru Speak

Ideas not coupled with action never become bigger than the brain cells they occupied.

—Arnold H. Glasgow

A business guru is someone who makes a pile of money out of telling people how to run a business. Often there's nothing new being offered and what they say is just common sense repackaged as a form of entertainment. Many will earn fortunes appearing at company conferences, holding seminars, and of course from writing the obligatory business book.

Some combine quasireligious and strong motivational techniques with the sort of language this book is devoted to, and whether they know it or not, they are the inventors of much of the bullshit we find in offices today. It may not be their fault, as some of the fools who use their words have no clue what they mean. They just think they sound good.

How to Be a Business Guru . . .

1. You must have a track record in business, or at least be able to fake one.
2. You should look good in a suit and have the ability to talk loudly. Alternatively you have to come across as

humble, as though you have had a great epiphany and want to share it with the world.

3. Great presentational skills are an absolute must. Rely on religious zeal and shouting if all else fails.

4. The right accent is essential, Southern or British is perfect, and you must be forceful and loud.

5. Find an original angle on the material. If in doubt steal someone else's ideas and repackage them as your own using different words.

6. Publish a book. It has to have a wacky title such as *How Red Are Your Toenails?* or *The Man Who Mistook His Company for a Vibrator* or an aggressive title like *Losing Is for Suckers You Sucker.* The book must be expensive and contain lots of charts, diagrams, and illustrations; big font size is also useful if you haven't got much to say.

7. Hire a good PR company to start the media circus rolling.

8. Lastly, find an audience.

Guru Words and Phrases

The guru is a rare breed, but they are the heroes and inspiration of most bullshitters. Here are some of the best phrases that have been hijacked by the corporate fake.

Action

MEANING: To do something, the general cry is "Who is going to action this?" instead of "Who is going to do this?"

BULLSHIT: Using words slightly differently than their original use is a prime feature of business bullshit. The word "action" sounds like a much better word to use in this context because it implies professionalism, and a "can-do" attitude.

Always On

MEANING: Ever alert, ready for action.

BULLSHIT: "Imagine that executive," says the guru. "Eyes bright, expression expectant, positive body language, committed, ready for business . . . he's always on and you should be too." "Fuck off!" thinks at least half the audience.

Barriers

MEANING: Something or someone who gets in the way.

BULLSHIT: Gurus love talking about barriers as a nonaggressive term applied to people who don't agree with the objective at hand. "Breaking down the barriers" generally means pushing through something at the expense of others. For bullshitters it's less threatening than "someone should be fired" but that's what the bullshitter implies by it.

Big Picture

MEANING: The wider view, the whole thing.

BULLSHIT: Management will say "You're not getting the bigger picture," implying that they are somehow aware of facts that you're not, or that the point you're making is so trivial, it's meaningless to someone as important as them. This is used especially in situations where the manager's plans are in fact insane.

Call to Action

MEANING: An encouragement or inducement to do something.

BULLSHIT: The guru will say that his or her session is a "call to action." In reality it's a symptom of the desperate management who need something to happen to save them or their company. Usually in response to some event like a poor sales period the "call to action" will go out to employees who will be expected to work their asses off to save the day. A great bullshit term, as by implication the "caller" is not the one who does the work.

Closure

MEANING: Finished, ended.

BULLSHIT: Achieving closure on a sale or a project is something gurus love; especially good fun is to talk in detail about the **path** to closure or the **journey.**

Competitive Advantage

MEANING: Business guru Michael Porter identified two types of competitive advantage. First, *cost advantage*, where the company delivers the same benefits but at lower cost. The second is *differentiation* where benefits are delivered that exceed those of your competitors.

BULLSHIT: The third advantage unidentified by Mr. Porter is the *bullshit advantage*, where the company that lies best about cost savings and benefits is the winner.

Conversation

MEANING: A spoken exchange.

BULLSHIT: A favorite of business gurus who talk about having "conversations" with customers and colleagues in an attempt to avoid conflict or provide something positive. It's forced and can be a little creepy when a colleague asks to have a "conversation" with you, especially if they mime quote marks as they say the word. Run!

Continuous Improvement

MEANING: An ongoing commitment to get better both as a company and as an individual.

BULLSHIT: At least one guru advocates this as a policy and it's been used by many a company president as an excuse for changing their business model, often controversially.

Disconnect
MEANING: A communications breakdown.

BULLSHIT: Nobody says "We haven't communicated properly." Instead, in the world of business bullshit people say "There's been a disconnect."

Empower
MEANING: Give someone the power to do something.

BULLSHIT: A watchword of a few years ago when business gurus were telling company bosses to empower their staff and "awaken the giant within." It's not much used nowadays, as management has realized that empowering staff is a very dangerous thing to do.

Energy
Oh, please! The worst bullshit word in the world. Anyone using it, saying they need it, saying you need it, or saying the company needs it, needs to be punished—very severely. It is almost guaranteed that the user will provoke the opposite reaction to the one intended.

Engage
MEANING: To draw someone in, to hold their attention. We need to "engage" our customers, or "engage" our teammates. You can't just talk to someone, you need to "engage" them in a **conversation.** That's how things get done.

BULLSHIT: A classic example of a guru telling us what we already know by making it into something that looks new.

Excellence

MEANING: Extremely high standards.

BULLSHIT: Another word that was bandied about in the '90s, usually along the lines of "a passion for excellence" or a "center of excellence." These days it seems to have been replaced by terms like **off the scale** and **outstanding**.

Focus

MEANING: A center of attention or activity, **in the spotlight, under the lens.**

BULLSHIT: Another classic, nearly all managers have used the word mainly when they think their teams have **taken their eyes off the ball**. You'll hear it in regards to being customer focused, team focused, client focused, career focused and on and on. Well, this book is bullshit focused, and the word should be banned.

Framework

MEANING: A structure around which a business plan or team is based.

BULLSHIT: Managers need something to build their plans with, and no matter how loose the framework, it is always trotted out as something to **hang things on**. Managers able to work in a fluid situation are viewed with suspicion by others, especially the company bullshitter who tends to need a rigid structure to climb up.

Future-Facing

MEANING: Always looking forward, always planning the future.

BULLSHIT: Gurus will tell companies to learn from the past but not emulate it; they must above all be future-facing. So don't do what those tossers did in the '90s, take on the assholes who are trying to grind you down now, identify those who could shaft you in the future, and get 'em.

Go for It

MEANING: This has to be lumped together with **energy** as one of those terms that when someone says it accompanied by a punch in the air, the automatic reaction in most people is to do the opposite. It's had its day, and the user is a little out of touch. Even the terms **kick ass, pump up the volume,** and **cook with gas** are out, especially when accompanied by **high-fives.** The modern bullshitter has more subtle methods to **rally the troops.**

BULLSHIT: Most managers who "go for it" see themselves as great leaders; managers who encourage others with the term are usually great avoiders.

Hedgehog Concept

MEANING: The hedgehog concept is an idea thought of by a person working independently that can change a company for the better and enhance that person's career in the process. While it stems from an essay written in the 1950s, many gurus have developed an ideology to encourage it.

BULLSHIT: A company bullshitter's nightmare.

Helicopter Vision

MEANING: Imagine a managing director "hovering" over the business watching events as they happen and taking action accordingly.

BULLSHIT: Great, but bear in mind that this could turn into **seagull vision**, where said manager flies over his staff, makes a loud noise and a great deal of commotion, shits on them occasionally, then takes off when the going gets tough.

Human Factor

MEANING: Human contribution, regardless if it's good or bad.

BULLSHIT: No matter how good the plans, there's always someone around who can fuck it up.

If You Keep Doing the Same Thing, the Same Thing Will Happen

MEANING: Well, duh! But it's remarkable how many people don't get this.

BULLSHIT: If you start hearing this at a company you're involved with, then pack your bags and go. It's especially worrisome when it becomes a mantra; then you know a lot of mistakes have been made.

Joined-Up Thinking

MEANING: When people have separate **conversations,** there are lots of ideas being created, and the process of gathering those ideas together to form a plan is called joined-up thinking.

BULLSHIT: This is the sort of self-complicating term that readily spouts from the mouths of gurus. Just *talk* to people, OK?

Lateral Thinking

MEANING: An unorthodox approach to problem-solving, from the work of the likes of Edward De Bono, lateral thinking is the process of problem-solving by looking at the issue from a different perspective.

BULLSHIT: So to do this, you have to **brainstorm, blue sky, think outside the box, stretch the envelope, get granular**, and go **deep diving**.

Leading Edge
MEANING: In the vanguard, the foremost in the market.

BULLSHIT: Type "leading edge" into Google, and twenty-five million responses appear. Gurus have for years encouraged companies to be one step ahead of their competition, to be **future-facing, innovative**, and to **lead the market**. Obviously some companies are claiming to be leading edge when they clearly aren't, so is it corporate bullshit or self-delusion?

Making a Difference
MEANING: Changing things, by implication for the better.

BULLSHIT: Young managers are often told to **make a mark**, but to the horror of most senior managers, gurus want them to actually **make a difference**. This is seen as threatening and unhealthy, as it could really jeopardize senior management's power.

Mission Statement
A true classic. Here's one for this book:

The purpose of this book is to highlight the use of bullshit in business and in other walks of life, with the aim of exposing and revealing fakes and bullshitters to the uninitiated, in a humorous and interesting way.

Virtually every large business has a mission statement in some form or another, basically to describe the purpose of the business. It's becoming unfashionable now as a term, replaced instead by **constitutions, manifestos,** and **articles**—in other words, more bullshit.

Missionwear

MEANING: Clothing, stationery, or anything that has the mission statement printed on it.

BULLSHIT: The worst sort of company propaganda. Beware anyone who is wearing it gladly.

Orchestra Model

MEANING: A scenario where the leader gives directions tailored to specific groups within the business, rather like a conductor leading an orchestra.

BULLSHIT: Something many gurus go on and on about when talking about management structures. It replaces the military-based hierarchy we're used to, but it could be efficient, and that's the scary thing about it.

Passion

MEANING: Excitement, eagerness, boundless enthusiasm.

BULLSHIT: Anyone who tells you that they're passionate about paper clips, widgets, spreadsheets, paperwork, or anything remotely boring is lying or crazy.

Proactive, Not Reactive

MEANING: This is anticipating and acting with forethought instead of waiting for something to happen before taking action.

BULLSHIT: One of many phrases used as a mantra by company senior management, usually it's a sign that something has already happened and it's all too late.

Pushing the Envelope/Stretching the Envelope

MEANING: The theory is that the envelope in question is a technical term relating to the performance of fighter aircraft. The envelope is the limits of the aircrafts' technical abilities.

BULLSHIT: A pretty odd way of saying "How can we do more?"

Raving Fans

MEANING: From a book by Kenneth Blanchard and Sheldon Bowles, a raving fan is a customer who is so overwhelmed by high levels of customer service that they brag about it and become part of the company "sales force."

BULLSHIT: Excellent opportunities for bullshitters. Customers like this are also considered the most gullible, as it takes a lot to shift their view even if bad service sets in.

Reality Check

MEANING: An assessment to determine if the circumstances or expectations conform to what's happening in real life.

BULLSHIT: For many companies, the real world is something that happens outside of the bubble in which they place themselves, and it can come as a big shock when something that they're convinced is right turns out to be totally wrong.

Reengineering

MEANING: This is the examination and then the modification of a company to change it for the better, including the implementation of the changes.

BULLSHIT: Change is always difficult. It means job losses, upheaval—a difficult period all around, though company leaders can't actually say that. Much better to "reengineer." That sounds much more professional.

Results-Driven, Outcome-Driven

MEANING: Geared toward a specific outcome. By implication this is done with high levels of concentration.

BULLSHIT: This attitude creates a culture dominated by insensitive, single-minded shits. You have been warned.

Rules of Engagement

MEANING: Companies are advised to understand any of the above before entering into negotiations, a trading period, or a new market.

BULLSHIT: Companies have a tendency not bother to find out what the parameters are before going **into battle**, which leaves others to clean up the mess.

Step Change

MEANING: A radical change, increase in pace.

BULLSHIT: Companies in trouble always talk about making step changes. Really what this means is that they're desperately looking for a **magic bullet** or **pot of gold** that could get them out of trouble.

Synergy

MEANING: Cooperative interaction among the departments or merged parts of a company, that creates something stronger and works to better effect.

BULLSHIT: One of the classic business guru words. Forgetting the **human factor**, they dream of organizations, corporations, and governments working in harmony to solve problems. If it weren't for real individuals complicating things, with synergy world famine could be eradicated, disease wiped out, war banished, and global warming a thing of the past . . . nice thought, though.

Theology

There have been many attempts to ally business culture to religious theology. One of the worst and probably most common is overemphasis on Good vs. Evil. One guru once asked, "Do you have any colleagues who are truly evil? Is there anything you can do about it?" Bullshitters beware!

The Seven Habits . . .

Mentioned often by managers who want to impress, from the book *The Seven Habits of Highly Effective People* by Stephen Covey, they are . . .

1. Be proactive
2. Begin with the end in mind
3. Put first things first
4. Think win-win
5. Seek first to understand, and then be understood
6. Synergize
7. Sharpen the saw

It may appear to be jargonized mumbo-jumbo to some, but they've sold some ten million copies, so there must be something in it. It is probably the most shown-off book in the office, and without even reading or understanding it people will quote from it and have it on their desk or on display somewhere just to look good. Woe betide any bullshitter who has a boss who has actually read and understood it.

This leads us neatly on to the Bullshitter's Bookshelf. . . .

The Bullshitter's Bookshelf

Looking good, giving the impression that he or she is up on all the latest management techniques, and boning up on all the latest buzzwords, the accomplished corporate bullshitter will have the appropriate books dotted around the office. Most business gurus and experts who write their ideas down mean well and some have something genuinely interesting and innovative to say. But when bullshitters are out to impress, it's about being seen with the right books, whether they understand them or not.

Here are the top ten most common books you'll find on a bullshitter's desk.

1. *Seven Habits of Highly Effective People* by Stephen Covey
   For those times when you really want to confuse your boss
2. *How to Win Friends and Influence People* by Dale Carnegie
   Top tips on how to get your own way
3. *The One Minute Manager* by Kenneth Blanchard and Spencer Johnson
   Bought by people who think management is easy
4. *Who Moved My Cheese?* by Spencer Johnson
   For those who want to pretend that they embrace change
5. *Winning* by Jack Welsh
   How it should be done . . .
6. *Getting Things Done* by David Allen
   A bullshitter's nightmare because it actually shows how to do things properly
7. *Fish!* by Harry Paul, Stephen Lundin, and John Christensen
   An uplifting and much quoted parable about fishmongers . . . it's very short
8. *Emotional Intelligence* by Daniel Goleman
   One of the best, most popular, and least read books
9. *Art of War* by Sun Tzu
   The one to be seen with . . .
10. *Feel the Fear and Do It Anyway* by Susan Jeffers
    The one they really read and then hide away . . .

BULLSHIT BINGO—Guru Speak

PASSION	BARRIERS	ENGAGE	FOCUS	REENGINEER-ING	JOINED-UP THINKING	RULES . . .	ENERGY
RESULTS-DRIVEN	EXCELLENCE	ALWAYS ON	EMPOWER	GO FOR IT	HEDGEHOG CONCEPT	PROACTIVE	COMPETITIVE ADVANTAGE
CLOSURE	CALL TO ACTION	FRAMEWORK	BIG PICTURE	CHANGE	LEADING EDGE	CONTINUOUS IMPROVE-MENT	GETTING THINGS DONE
FOCUS	HUMAN FACTOR	CONNECT	VISION	INNOVATION	LATERAL THINKING	DRIVEN	MANIFESTO
REALITY CHECK	ORCHESTRA MODEL	DISCONNECT	MISSION-WEAR	MAKE A DIFFERENCE	REINVENTING	STEP CHANGE	STRETCH THE ENVELOPE
ACTION	SYNERGY	THEOLOGY	FUTURE-FACING	HELICOPTER VISION	CONVER-SATION	OUTCOME-DRIVEN	MISSION STATEMENT

How to play: Simply check off 6 words or phrases in one meeting and shout out BINGO

7. Consultant Bullshit

A businessman and a consultant had a meeting; the businessman asked what the consultant's rates would be for the suggested project.

"We structure the project up front and charge $5,000 initially, for three questions," replied the consultant.

"Isn't that pretty steep?" asked the businessman.

"Yes, it is," the consultant replied, "and what was your third question?"

Consultants can bullshit with the best of them. There are plenty of expressions in this book commonly used by them, but here are a few that they really popularized.

Dog and Pony Show
MEANING: An over-the-top presentation.

BULLSHIT: In other words, the usual PowerPoint presentation with the usual bullshit.

Holistic
MEANING: Taking in the whole picture.

BULLSHIT: A classic bit of consultant bullshit, taking a holistic approach means encompassing all aspects of the project. It will also take the most time and make them more money as a consequence.

Put Flesh on the Bones

MEANING: Add more detail.

BULLSHIT: Consultants just love this request, as it allows them to pad their work to make it last longer and appear more authoritative, earning more cash in the process.

Scope

MEANING: Range, size.

BULLSHIT: The bigger the scope of the job, the bigger the contract.

Squaring the Circle

MEANING: Trying to do the impossible.

BULLSHIT: Sometimes people use **circling the square**; either way in my opinion it's pretty damn confusing.

Presentations

PowerPoint is the main tool of bullshit for the consultant, and of course any bullshitter worth his salt would include a chart within a presentation. Here are the most common.

THE BOSTON BOX

Developed by the Boston Consultancy Group, this classic device always goes a long way to impress a potential client, officially known as the Growth-Share matrix, it evaluates a company's products by share and growth potential.

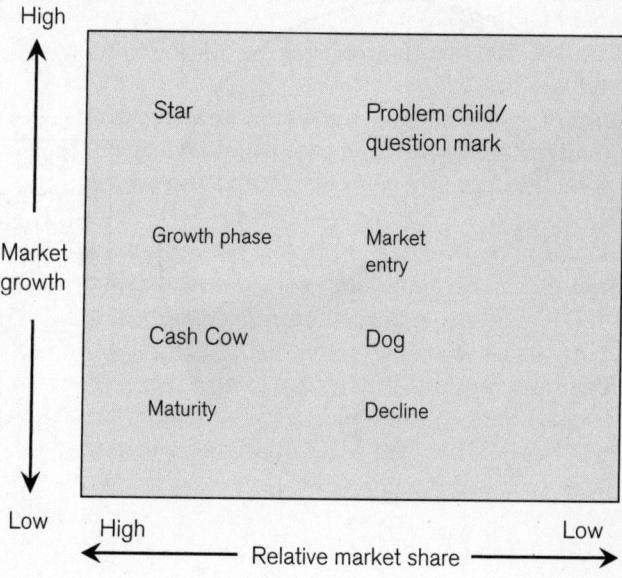

PIE CHARTS

Another bullshit presentation classic, a way of showing portions and ratios.

The Lying Pie Chart

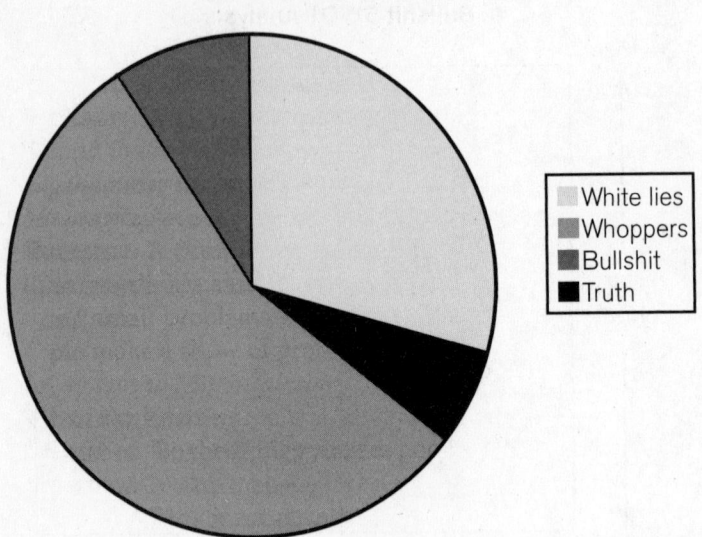

SWOT Analysis

It has to be done at the beginning of any bit of company analysis for every strategy; you can bet it will end up geared so that the consultant will profit.

Bullshit SWOT Analysis

Strengths	Weaknesses
Make the user sound important Makes things sound good and gives impression that things are better than reality	Overuse threatens credibility User must have good acting ability and strong memory
Improved career prospects Improved sex life More success	Being found out The truth
Opportunities	Threats

Venn Diagram

Great for comparisons and finding out what things have in common.

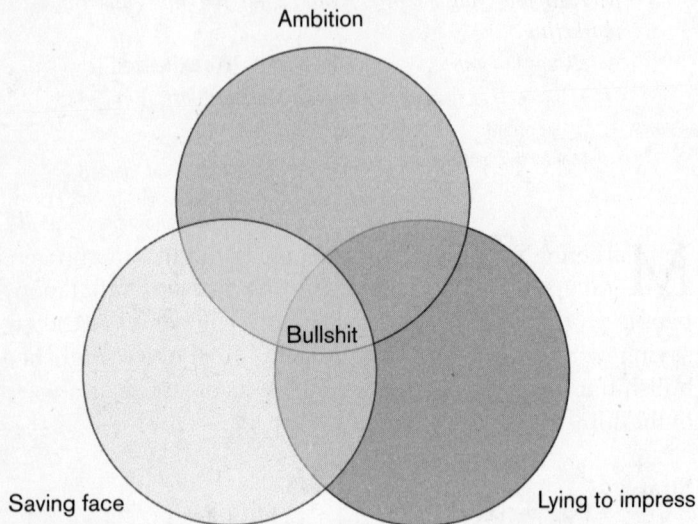

The Bullshit Venn

8. Marketing and Advertising

Me? In love with a pig? Wait 'till I tell the guys in marketing.

—Kermit the Frog
The Muppets Take Manhattan (1984)

Marketing and advertising are rife with bullshit and general up-its-own-ass nonsense. The problem is that many people working in these areas actually believe what they're saying without knowing it's bullshit. To the accomplished bullshitter this is a paradise where lovers of jargon and users of the silky tongue will shine.

Strategy

Many managing directors set the **strategy** (the plan for doing something) themselves, others employ strategy directors, whose only role appears to be to organize the company conference where other people's ideas are delivered, often reworked as their own.

Marketing Directors often set strategy based on **market research**, employing specialist companies and legions of consultants to tell them about their own company and **the market** they're working in. Usually any long-standing employee will know as much.

The words *strategy* and *strategic* are used to cover a multitude of sins, and here are just a few of them:

Strategic Direction—where we think we're going

Strategic Approach—how we think we're going to go about it

Strategic Fit—those who are going with us

Strategic Goals—what we think we're going to get

Strategic Plan—how we think we're going to get there

Strategic Thinking—real issues aside, how can we make ourselves look good?

There are various types of strategies:

High-risk Strategy—don't blame us if it goes wrong

Low-risk Strategy—it won't go wrong

Exit Strategy—for when it does all go wrong

Development Strategy—We think we know what to do, but we'll take it slowly in case it's wrong. This is common in government.

Short-term Strategy—Get it done before we get fired. For most listed companies this is a way of life.

Long-term Strategy—There's no hurry; by the time anything is implemented, the whole situation will have changed anyway.

Here's a classic from the UK government's own Strategy Survival Guide.

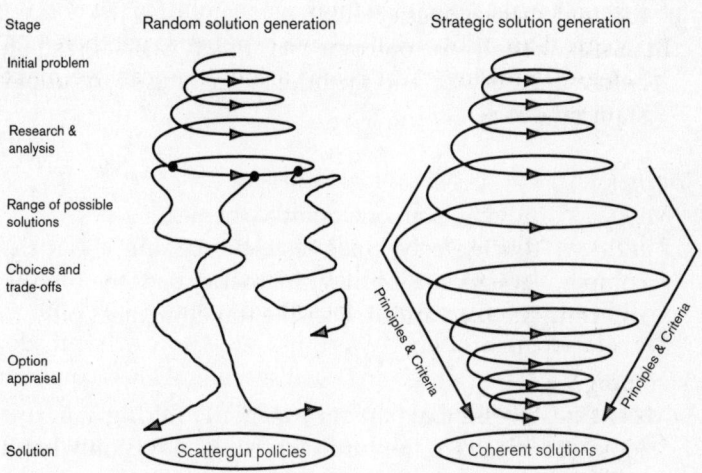

Armed with this information, the company strategy will be formed, but not before lots of the following bull.

Acorns, Seeds

MEANING: Ideas, especially new ones.

BULLSHIT: There are actually no new ideas, only those that are approved of.

Blue-Sky Thinking

MEANING: An attempt to tackle an issue or come up with a new strategy or approach by thinking differently, without boundaries and constraints.

BULLSHIT: If only that were really true . . .

Brainstorm
> MEANING: A meeting where free and original thinking is encouraged to solve a problem or to come up with a strategy. In less aggressive companies it's also known as a **thought shower**, bless them.
>
> BULLSHIT: Usually the outcome has already been agreed on before the meeting, and the brainstorm is used to **rubber stamp** the idea.

Journey
> MEANING: Moving from one point to the next.
>
> BULLSHIT: Touchy-feely types just love talking about the company going on a journey, the **rocky road**, the **bumpy ride**, and the **road ahead**. Pass the travel sickness pills.

Visioning
> MEANING: An essential part of **Strategic Thinking**, it means looking forward to the future, trying to envision what it will be.
>
> BULLSHIT: Look back at previous plans and see where it's got them.

Customers, Clients, and Consumers

Any customer-based strategy works on anticipating the future needs and demands of customers; the people whom the employees ultimately work for. Here are a few of the choicest terms companies use to convince themselves that they're offering the ultimate customer service.

Client-Focused
> MEANING: A process, mainly used in the business-to-business (**B2B**) world where a company delivers new products and

services to their clients based on a thorough understanding of their actual needs.

BULLSHIT: Yeah right. Sounds good, though. See also **consumer-facing**.

Connect

MEANING: To talk, make contact.

BULLSHIT: "We must *connect* with our customers" or "I'm not feeling any connection with you" are terms generally used by people who have no clue how to communicate properly and are usually mystified by the fact that others don't agree with their point of view. Using the word in conversation signifies the most desperate and least socially adjusted of your colleagues. They are to be avoided—disconnected, in fact.

Consumer Agenda

MEANING: What the customers want, what they plan to buy. Predicting what's on their consumers' agenda is for most companies their main preoccupation.

BULLSHIT: Many careers are built by people who manage to kid their colleagues and bosses that they know what customers want. A classic consultant's term.

Consumer-Facing

MEANING: A company is consumer-facing when it works in direct contact with its customers, being aware of their needs and delivering a particular service. Many Web sites are considered consumer-facing.

BULLSHIT: Who the hell are they kidding? Many companies will convince themselves they are consumer-facing when in fact they are profit-facing. See also **client-focused**.

Consumer Intuitive
MEANING: Being instinctively aware of what your customer wants instinctively without thought.

BULLSHIT: If you can achieve this, you're a genius and you won't need to bullshit at all.

Customer Obsessed
MEANING: Knowing about customers' needs and likely requirements to the point of obsession.

BULLSHIT: Companies will say they are customer or consumer obsessed and talk about giving them what they want. In reality all companies are out to make a profit and will always hold something back. What this really means is "giving customers as much as we can get away with so that they give us more money than our competitors."

Educating Customers
MEANING: Persuading customers to part with their cash is an industry in itself and many companies spend fortunes on consultants and business gurus to get the secret to success. Some firms will attempt to change their customers' habits by using techniques such as incentives and advertising. In other words, **changing customer behavior** to their advantage.

BULLSHIT: Customers are stupid; they are only there to be taken advantage of, to further enhance careers.

Empathy
MEANING: Being on the customers' side, being aware of their needs in a sympathetic and thoughtful way.

BULLSHIT: In this context it's about companies faking empathy with the customer, so that customers then become loyal spenders, leading to bigger profits and more bull-shit. See **raving fans**.

Top of Mind
MEANING: High priority, the product most people think of first in a given situation.

BULLSHIT: A sort of nirvana for most companies when they can prove that their products are the first for consumers. It's staying there that's the problem, and that's when the bullshit kicks in.

Advertising and Promotion
No other area in business attracts more bullshit and bull-shitters than this, but most fakes are out for themselves and will be treating customers and colleagues with the usual dis-guised contempt. They will talk about the **four Ps** (price, place, product, and promotion), but much of what's sug-gested will be advertising **puffery**—in other words, just sub-jective opinions and superlatives.

So here are the key bullshit words. Make sure you stay **on message** with these, the company bullshitter will be **well up to speed** . . .

Bells and Whistles
MEANING: It does everything.

BULLSHIT: It [the deal or product] comes with everything in-cluded and more. Whoever says this is usually holding something back; be suspicious.

Call to Action
MEANING: An encouragement or inducement to do some-thing, such as respond to an ad or click on the button that says "click here."

BULLSHIT: Some managers use this term in a more general sense when dealing with their staff; it means they want someone else to do the work.

Demographics

MEANING: The study of the characteristics of a consumer population or portion thereof, otherwise known as a **segment**.

BULLSHIT: With its pseudoscientific overtones, this term is perfect bullshit material. Be seen to be an expert on the key demographics to your company, and you'll be seen as a bit of a genius. The company bullshitter knows this and will want to give that impression.

Differentiation

MEANING: Many small companies can't compete with larger ones, especially on pricing, so they will concentrate on what makes them different. Company presidents will sometimes use it as a watchword, particularly if they operate in a market where they're up against stiff competition.

BULLSHIT: The marketing bullshitter uses this term when in meetings with the finance department, as it gives the impression that they're being prudent. The term **point of difference** is used in the same context.

Door Opener

MEANING: Something in an ad or promotion that starts the **conversation** with the customer. That is, after a **connection** with them has taken place.

BULLSHIT: "Once the door is open, you are mine . . ."

Elasticity
MEANING: Generally it's applied to the relationship between the price of a product and its sales; the lower the price, the higher the sales. Conversely when the price goes up, sales go down—as though the relationship were elastic. Cigarette sales are inelastic because no matter how much the price goes up, the poor addicted suckers keep buying them.

BULLSHIT: One of the great excuse words in marketing for the times when sales don't come through or their ad is a dog.

Feel-Good Factor
MEANING: It's important that customers feel good about the products they buy and the companies that sell them, and executives will take care that any message or promotion signed off on will have the right feel-good factor.

BULLSHIT: It's an important part of the company bullshitters' strategy too, as the last thing they want is for their boss to have anything other than positive feelings toward them.

Going Viral
MEANING: State of bliss for most advertisers is when their ad is so popular, it gets sent from office to office and friend to friend via the Internet.

BULLSHIT: Well, bullshit is viral in many ways. . . .

Hype
MEANING: Inflated overpromotion, extra exposure—derived from the word *hypodermic*.

BULLSHIT: Hype is the lifeblood of every bullshitter.

Impactful

MEANING: Promotions and advertising campaigns must have the right level of impact on those who they're aimed at. You'll hear managers often drone on about **impactful** displays and offers.

BULLSHIT: This isn't even a proper word; it's one purely designed to make the user look good.

Inspirational

MEANING: In this context, we want you to be so inspired by our products that you spend your money on them.

BULLSHIT: Telling you what we think you want to hear, in the hope you'll spend some money on our products.

Market Leading

MEANING: Most companies dream of leading their chosen market, some dominant ones actually do, while others claim to widen or change the market with their latest products or campaigns. In reality it often has more to do with economic factors than marketing bullshit.

BULLSHIT: Many companies kid themselves and their staff that they are market leading when in fact they are being complacent.

Market Segments

MEANING: Portions of a particular market based on age, wealth, region, gender, etc.

BULLSHIT: The bullshitter will know their market segments, from **ABC1's** to **D's** and **E's**, to **Fit Grays** and **Aspiring Sophisticates**, even **Slobs**. The cleverer sounding the term, the more likely the bullshitter is to use it because it makes them seem brighter. A colleague once attempted to impress the managing director with his knowledge of market segments. "Which segment do I fit into?" she asked. He looked at his sheet and without thinking he said, "walking corpses." He no longer works for that company.

Market Share

MEANING: The proportion of market dominance achieved by a company.

BULLSHIT: Bullshitters will use market share as a badge, but it's risky because the market has **elasticity** and a price hike or a poor promotion could ruin it for them.

Mechanics and Vehicles

Some would be forgiven in thinking that a conversation overheard in a marketing department could be about cars, but a **vehicle** is the medium by which the promotional **message** is put across. While the term **mechanic** is actually the promotion itself, whether it is a 3-for-2 or a price cut.

Mega, Monster

MEANING: Huge, extra, more.

BULLSHIT: No promotion or campaign simply does well, it has to be mega. Monster, on the other hand, is bigger than mega—it is extra huge!

Mind Food

MEANING: Books, newspapers, and magazines are really mind food to nourish our brains.

BULLSHIT: If you believe that, you'll believe anything . . . and your mind is probably dog food.

Must

MEANING: Obligation, a requirement and inevitability.

BULLSHIT: An interesting change of meaning here as things become "a must" or "must-have" item—a marketing manager's dream.

Niche

MEANING: Niche marketing is in-vogue nowadays. Web sites and TV channels in particular go for ever-smaller groups, hoping to tap into their interests and the high spending power devotees have.

BULLSHIT: Niche groups are particularly open to exploitation because they spend more on their interests, but you need to be an expert to figure out what their interests are.

On Message

MEANING: Aware of what's going on, sticking to the company or party line.

BULLSHIT: Woe betide any bullshitter who goes **off message** and isn't aware of what the boss wants.

Package

MEANING: The "package" could be anything from a real box to a salary deal, but in this context the executive will be looking for a collection of ads, promotions, and marketing strategy which combined make the package.

BULLSHIT: The male bullshitter will talk about the size of the package as though it's something physical, and you can be sure there's an inverse relationship working in there somewhere.

Paradigm

MEANING: Taken from one of the major dictionaries: *A set of assumptions, concepts, values, and practices that constitutes a way of viewing reality for the community that shares them, especially in an intellectual discipline.* This book, then, is about the paradigm of bullshit. If it causes a change in the behavior of people and the way they use bullshit, then a **paradigm shift** will have taken place.

BULLSHIT: A word beloved by those who want to appear clever or well read in American business practices, they will talk about group and market paradigms without a clue what the word really means . . . but it *sounds* good.

Positioning

MEANING: Sometimes in marketing known as **placement**, it's where your product or company is placed in relation to other products and companies in the market.

BULLSHIT: Companies get very clever about product placement. For example, TV services being plugged in newspapers owned by the same company. For the competitive bullshitter as always it is about them and how they are positioned in relation to their colleagues.

Proposition

MEANING: The offer.

BULLSHIT: Marketing people like to use the term proposition because it has sexual overtones and they hope some of that will rub off on them.

Qualitative and Quantitative Research

MEANING: In qualitative research you seek out people's attitudes and preferences, usually by conducting unstructured interviews or focus groups. For example did Coca-Cola do enough qualitative research before they (disastrously for sales) changed the formula of Coke in the '80s?

In quantitative research you use measurement of consumer trends within a group. For example one of the biggest crimes for manufacturers is to launch a product without doing the research on how many people are likely to want to buy it.

BULLSHIT: Another pair of terms that are great for sounding good, but don't get them muddled up!

Sexy

MEANING: Advertising campaigns can be described as sexy—not those featuring Claudia Schiffer but those that do the job very successfully and create certain moist feelings about their products in those who buy them.

BULLSHIT: **Sex it up** or **sexing it up** is the first thing any bullshitter thinks of in most situations—anything to make them look better.

Solutions

MEANING: A term used to broaden the scope of a product or idea. So this book isn't a book to a retailer, it's a gift solution. An aspirin is a pain solution, a bed is a sleeping solution, and a grave is a burial solution and so on. Whole departments and businesses have been created using this way of thinking.

BULLSHIT: It's an effective lying solution.

Target

MEANING: To aim something such as an ad at a specific market.

BULLSHIT: Those doing their jobs will be targeting external

consumers and markets, while the company bullshitter will target their internal opposition.

The Customer Is Always Right

MEANING: A slogan attributed to H. Gordon Selfridge, the founder of the Selfridges store in Oxford Street, London, UK.

BULLSHIT: In reality it should be, "The customer is always right, providing it doesn't cost too much money."

Touchy-Feely, High Touch/Low Tech

MEANING: Close physically, emotional, open to feelings, easy to understand.

BULLSHIT: Artistic, marketing, and advertising people are renowned for their touchy-feely approach to work; this leaves the rest of the business distinctly uncomfortable and suspicious because they would, in general, like to leave their emotions hidden, thanks very much.

USP

MEANING: The **Unique Selling Point** for any company is essential to **differentiate** themselves from their competitors.

BULLSHIT: The company bullshitters will also have a USP to make them stand out, they will be known for something positive that will help their careers and keep them ahead of the competition.

Value Added

MEANING: Something of value given or included.

BULLSHIT: The trick is to appear to give a lot but not give much.

Water-Cooler Campaign

MEANING: Something that is so exciting it's discussed in the office the next day around the water coolers where everyone congregates.

BULLSHIT: When have you ever seen people hanging around water coolers? It doesn't happen! OK, maybe the odd sad guy is there, in the hope someone young and attractive might appear.

Wavelength

MEANING: In harmony, several departments working well together on the same thing, see also **on message**.

BULLSHIT: Would bullshitters be on the same wavelength as us when reading this book? Probably not; they'd use it as a personal bullshit manual.

Winning Hearts and Minds

MEANING: Persuading, bringing people to your side by doing good.

BULLSHIT: A term made popular by Bush and his team. They did it before the election, they did it before the war and to the Iraqis during the war, and there's a bullshitter doing it to you.

Wordsmith

MEANING: A fluent writer, to edit a text to improve it.

BULLSHIT: The top bullshitter will never let something (especially with their name on it) go before a superior or the public without signing off on it and ensuring it says exactly what it should. They don't *edit* though, they *wordsmith*.

Wow Factor
> MEANING: Something in a campaign, product, or idea that makes you go "Wow!"
>
> BULLSHIT: Advertisers and their clients will always be looking to add that certain something to whatever they are selling; some call it an extra layer of bullshit.

The Brand

Brand image is incredibly important to any company, and the image that their brand projects can make or break them. For example, UK jewelry retailer Gerald Ratner once made a famous speech in which he stated that what he sold was "crap." He destroyed the dream for many who had bought jewelry in his stores.

The brand is often well used by company leaders as an effective way to give their employees a sense of focus and belonging. As for Ratner, his business suffered accordingly after his speech and it is seen as one of the biggest business errors and a lesson to us all. In other words, you need at least a little bullshit to survive; it doesn't pay to be too honest.

Here are some terms to watch out for.

Badge Item
> MEANING: A piece of clothing or product that says something about your lifestyle and values.
>
> BULLSHIT: Advertisers kill to get this level of acceptance for their products; meanwhile the company bullshitters will be picking the right badge items to make them look good around the office.

Brandalism, Brandroid
> You know who they are—Formula 1 cars, burger chains, and many more, all guilty of overusing their brands, put-

ting them everywhere on their products and in their advertising. This is called **Brandalism.**

A **Brandroid** is someone who has bought the company line completely, who then automatically spouts company slogans and lives life according to the values of the company. Usually sad individuals who should know better, and in their heart of hearts they probably do.

Brandwidth
MEANING: The level of recognition awarded to a product within a market.

BULLSHIT: The level of recognition awarded to the bullshitter within their office—probably should be called *bullwidth.*

Iconic
MEANING: An iconic brand is Coca-Cola. They have heritage, huge sales, and popularity plus a global reach.

BULLSHIT: Many companies kid themselves that their brand fits into this category, and many a strategy has gone awry because they have underestimated the general apathy of the general public. Celebrities have a similar issue, many acting like they are A-list **icons** when they're definitely not. The amazing thing is that we let them get away with it.

Off Brand
MEANING: Not advertised with the correct values, or unsympathetic to the brand.

BULLSHIT: As with **off message**, it's a desperate situation when your advertising company advertises your product as something it's not and with values you don't subscribe to. Bullshitters beware.

BULLSHIT BINGO—Marketing

PARADIGM	MARKET SEGMENT	BRAND IMAGE	USP	WOW FACTOR	INSPIRA-TIONAL	IMPACTFUL	VALUE ADDED
ICONIC	MEGA	ENERGY	DEMO-GRAPHICS	CONNECT	CONSUMER-FACING	POSITIONING	MUST
CONSUMER AGENDA	ELASTICITY	SOLUTION	ON MESSAGE	BRAINSTORM	HYPE	THE BRAND	ALIGN
BLUE SKY	GOING VIRAL	FEEL GOOD FACTOR	HOLISTIC	MECHANIC	EMPOWER	FOCUS	WINNING HEARTS AND MINDS
VEHICLE	TARGET	CUSTOMER	LOYALTY	INSPIRE	MARKET LEADING	PROPOSITION	POINT OF DIFFERENCE
PACKAGE	NICHE	VISIONING	EMPATHY	CALL TO ACTION	BELLS AND WHISTLES	MONSTER	TOUCHY-FEELY

How to play: Simply check off 6 words or phrases in one meeting and shout out BINGO!

Conference Bullshit

Conferences are essentially all about bullshit, where the company president will tell you how the corporation is doing, choosing each word carefully, politically, often being completely over the top and behaving in an unnaturally confident and happy way.

It's a time when heads of departments give their presentations, when management comes across all motivational, and there's very little real honesty.

Microsoft PowerPoint is the bullshitter's tool of choice, as it can be used to hide all sorts of problems. Watch out for people whose graphs and figures can't be read, or who have more than five bullet points to a slide and more pictures than words; they're probably bullshitting about something.

The words and phrases used in conferences are spread throughout this book, but there's one area of bullshit unique to them and that's the music that's used to heighten the atmosphere and create the right mood.

Here are our top ten conference tunes, designed to set the mood and rally the troops.

1. "Simply the Best"—Tina Turner
2. "We Are the Champions"—Queen
3. "Ready to Go"—Republica
4. "Chariots of Fire"—Vangelis
5. "Beautiful Day"—U2
6. "Rebel Rebel"—David Bowie
7. "Born to Run"—Bruce Springsteen
8. "Fanfare for the Common Man"—Aaron Copeland
9. "Eye of the Tiger"—Survivor
10. "Money"—Pink Floyd

See the conference music bingo card; let us know your conference heroes.

BULLSHIT BINGO—Conference Music

"FANFARE FOR THE COMMON MAN" COPELAND	THE JAMES BOND THEME TUNE	"READY TO GO" REPUBLICA	"BOYS ARE BACK IN TOWN" THIN LIZZIE	"AMERICA" NEIL DIAMOND	"WITH A LITTLE HELP FROM MY FRIENDS" BEATLES	"THRILLER" MICHAEL JACKSON	"CHARIOTS OF FIRE" VANGELIS	"MONEY FOR NOTHING" DIRE STRAITS	"(I CAN'T GET NO) SATISFACTION" THE ROLLING STONES
"CARS" GARY NUMAN	"JUMP" VAN HALEN	"EVERYBODY WANTS TO RULE THE WORLD" TEARS FOR FEARS	"IN THE AIR TONIGHT" PHIL COLLINS	"TUBTHUMPING" CHUMBAWAMBA	"I CAN SEE CLEARLY NOW" JOHNNY NASH	"R-E-S-P-E-C-T" ARETHA FRANKLIN	"BORN TO RUN" BRUCE SPRINGSTEEN	"SIMPLY THE BEST" TINA TURNER	"EVERY LITTLE THING SHE DOES IS MAGIC" POLICE
THEME SONG FROM ROCKY	"BEAUTIFUL DAY" U2	"JUMPIN' JACK FLASH" ROLLING STONES	"WE ARE THE CHAMPIONS" QUEEN	"WHAT A WONDERFUL WORLD" LOUIS ARMSTRONG	"SMOKE ON THE WATER" DEEP PURPLE	"REBEL REBEL" DAVID BOWIE	"THANK YOU" DIDO	"SUCCESS" DURAN DURAN	"THE WORLD IS NOT ENOUGH" GARBAGE
"MY HEART WILL GO ON" CELINE DION	"WHEN YOU BELIEVE" WHITNEY HOUSTON AND MARIAH CAREY	"EYE OF THE TIGER" SURVIVOR	"WELCOME TO THE JUNGLE" GUNS N' ROSES	"MONEY" PINK FLOYD	"THE POWER OF THE DREAM" CELINE DION	"ALL YOU NEED IS LOVE" BEATLES	"IT'S A KIND OF MAGIC" QUEEN	"GOOD THING" FINE YOUNG CANNIBALS	"I BELIEVE I CAN FLY" R. KELLY

How to play: Simply check off 4 songs in one conference and shout out BINGO!

9. Human Resources and People

I wish all the people who have trouble communicating would just shut up.

—Tom Lehrer

Sometimes known as the People Team, the HR department manages recruitment and handles dismissals and layoffs plus a whole host of issues in between. You have to feel sympathy for them, as they must receive more bullshit than most, but as you'll see they're often the best at it giving it too.

The **Peter Principle** states that employees within an organization will advance to their highest level of competence and then be promoted to and remain at a level at which they are incompetent. It is amazing how true this is and how those who were fantastic as a worker are often basically incompetent as a manager.

The common denominator is people; once the worker becomes a manager, the whole dynamic changes and bullshit comes into play.

HR Vocabulary

There's a language used here to soften blows, to take out confrontation, and prepare people for the worst . . . otherwise known as HRPR.

Here are some terms you may be familiar with.

Assessment, Appraisal, Review

MEANING: Workers are scored on a set of criteria to determine their progress, objectives, and training needs.

BULLSHIT: The lifeblood of HR, the time when all the bullshitting and planning come together, the time to shine, the time to set easy objectives for the next review.

Between Jobs

MEANING: The period between finishing one job and starting another.

BULLSHIT: In reality, there's not another.

Career Planning

MEANING: Planning the long-term career, with personal needs in mind as well as the company's.

BULLSHIT: On joining a company bullshitters will know largely what jobs they'll want to aim for and plan accordingly. Those naïve enough to believe their managers have their careers at heart will be sorely treated. The number 1 rule in career planning is look after number 1.

Check In/Check Out

MEANING: In some companies the caring world of HR is a little extreme; before any meeting happens, people are asked to check-in their feelings at the beginning and check-out their feelings at the end.

BULLSHIT: Thinking "Oh, for God's sake, just get on with it!!" while saying "I feel really privileged to work for this company."

Coaching
MEANING: A recent trend is to have a coach, usually an experienced ex-businessperson who will help company managers to become better at their jobs.
BULLSHIT: Bullshitting seems to require no coaching.

Collegial
MEANING: Able to work well with others.
BULLSHIT: Appearing to be able to work well with others.

Core Competences
MEANING: The things you know how to do, the things you're good at.
BULLSHIT: With seemingly supernatural abilities the company bullshitter will seem to know exactly which areas it's worth being good at and what not to bother with.

Cream Always Rises to the Top
MEANING: The best people always rise to the top echelons of the business.
BULLSHIT: Shit floats too.

Dedicated Resource
MEANING: A person or team working on a specific project or role.
BULLSHIT: A good way of justifying the expansion of a team, a dedicated resource is needed for each specific task. The idea is to get a bigger team with higher costs, so that a pay raise request is justified for the extra responsibility.

Dotted Line
MEANING: Part of the reporting structure in a large organization where someone, while not being the boss, still has

control over another's work, hence a dotted line responsibility.

BULLSHIT: Great for the company bullshitters, because it enables them to play the dotted lines against the real boss, to the bullshitter's benefit of course.

Downtime

MEANING: A period of time when something, either a system or factory, isn't operating, for example, when tools are downed.

BULLSHIT: This probably isn't a good thing but is always a good opportunity to improve scores at Minesweeper.

A Fish Rots from the Head Down

MEANING: Basically a reference to the performance of the head of a company, the implication being that if they leave, the company will flounder (geddit?).

BULLSHIT: It works another way; since a company head's influence on some companies is so great, if they are poor leaders then the whole business will suffer.

Golden Handcuffs, Golden Handshake, Golden Hello, Golden Parachute

MEANING: A good thing, whatever the situation, as it means a payment of some description and an incentive to stay or go.

BULLSHIT: The company bullshitters will position themselves at the front of the line regardless.

Knowledge Workers

MEANING: People who actually know what they are doing and have some skills.

BULLSHIT: People whose chameleon-like skills enable them to look like they know what they're doing.

Learning Curve
MEANING: A graphic depiction of the rate of learning, of progress in learning a skill against the time required to master it.

BULLSHIT: At the start this imaginary curve is very steep; as experience is gained, it flattens out to a shallow incline. It doesn't seem to register apathy, though.

Mentoring
MEANING: The process of senior managers guiding the junior executives' careers.

BULLSHIT: It has the potential to be a bit like thieves turning out to be better thieves after serving time in prison.

Objective
MEANING: Target, outcome.

BULLSHIT: Usually given as part of the **appraisal** procedure, the trick is to get easy objectives while the person setting them thinks they're hard.

One Team
MEANING: The motivational side of HR will always try to break down barriers between departments and teams, mainly using the "We're all one team" mantra.

BULLSHIT: It doesn't work of course, but everyone pretends it does.

Open-Door Policy
MEANING: The HR department wants to give the impression that they are always accessible and available to solve problems.

BULLSHIT: An opportunity to get the gossip and spread it.

Partnership
MEANING: HR departments always work in "partnership" with their colleagues.

BULLSHIT: Company bullshitters look like they work in partnership but are out for themselves.

Personal Growth
MEANING: Getting more mature, acquiring knowledge and skills.

BULLSHIT: Despite appearances and what is said, this is actually a personal responsibility; don't expect too much company support.

Rank and Yank
MEANING: A relatively new term said to originate from the debacle at Enron. People are ranked according to results, with the worst performers being "yanked" out of the business.

BULLSHIT: The culture this creates is made for the bullshitter, who will lie, brown-nose, and back-stab his or her way up the ranking.

Skill Set
MEANING: The skills you have.

BULLSHIT: The skills you want to give the impression you have.

Square Peg in a Round Hole
MEANING: A person whose skills and job role don't match.

BULLSHIT: Usually most of the senior management in any company.

Structure

MEANING: Every business has a structure and a hierarchy, and it's usually the job of the HR team to administer it. There are **flat structures**, where hierarchy is minimized, and optimal **restructures** geared to efficiency.

BULLSHIT: The weak personalities will end up with smaller jobs and smaller teams, the **big guns** will get bigger teams and bigger offices, the clever company bullshitters will work within this framework giving the impression their needs are paramount.

Succession Planning

MEANING: Plans are made so that when one person leaves a job, another is ready to step in.

BULLSHIT: The reality is that it never really happens, as opinions on people change daily and either staff turnover is too high or too low to make it work effectively.

Teambuilding

MEANING: Many managers really care about how their teams work with each other; it's a real science to some. Often this aspect is delegated to the HR folk, who will organize **off sites**, where the team works on a series of exercises designed to get them working together in **harmony**.

BULLSHIT: Yeah, right.

Virtual Team, Virtual Manager

MEANING: A group of people who work on one thing, the difference being that they don't go to a physical office, they work remotely and are managed remotely too.

BULLSHIT: A good opportunity to dodge work.

Getting the Boot—the Bullshit Terms

We all know instances where companies have informed their staff of their loss of employment in the media, even via text message, and here are some of the most common terms. Essentially they all add up to the same thing . . . you're out.

Ax, bust, chop, cut, fire, terminate—Indicates a forced removal, usually on the grounds of some sort of misconduct.

Canning, canned, ditch, sack—Indicates that the person being **shown the door** is something to be ashamed of, the company concerned doesn't want to **air their dirty laundry in public**.

Constructive dismissal, forced resignation—Some managers have this down to a fine art, making their employees' lives hell so that they leave "voluntarily," saving the manager from paying them off. It's difficult to prove and fraught with bullshit.

Derecruit, downsize, reengineer, restructure, right-size—All terms used to make the fact that a company is sacking lots of people more palatable and to give the impression that more is being done aside from just sacking.

Dismissed, get the boot, marching orders—More militaristic overtones and the impression that there is a lack of honor in the leaving of the person being sacked.

Drinking at the last chance saloon—This is a period usually prior to the event and unbeknownst to the person being sacked.

I want him/her out—The cry of a manager desperate to get rid of someone, usually to the HR team who then have to facilitate the exit, usually by transferring the person but occasionally by more devious means: "Go now with a good reference or later with a bad one."

Lay off, let go—An attempt to soften the blow by softening the words—it doesn't work.

Redundancy—The process by which companies reduce their staff; for some this carries the wrong overtones who prefer it all to be voluntary or to have it said that they resign.

Resign—To chuck in your job and go to work for someone else can be very satisfying, until you realize you're just listening to the same old bullshit.

Recruitment Bullshit

Open the papers at the classifieds, and bullshit abounds. Here are some of the job ad favorites and what they really mean.

Achievement oriented—Thank God, because we don't give a shit.

Clarity of vision—Because we haven't a clue what to do next.

Commercial acumen—We need someone who knows what a P&L is.

Communication skills—No one is talking to each other and we need you to mediate.

Decision maker—We need someone to blame.

Development—Get them before they develop enough skills to be classed as a senior manager; they're cheaper.

Dynamic—Well, someone needs to do the work.

Energetic—Now that you've finished that, the boss's car needs washing.

Enthusiastic—We need someone who likes our ideas.

Exciting—Because we aren't, we're boring.

Flair—Because we don't want another boring git.

Highly organized—Thank God, because we're in a mess.

Innovative—We don't want boring people in our company. Also read as young.

Interpersonal skills—Someone who can actually talk to other people without embarrassment or being embarrassing.

Leading—Well we are; in Berkshire.

Lifestyle—No working-class people need apply.

Make a difference—Because we've run out of ideas.

Money motivated—Low salary, high bonus, unachievable targets.

Negotiation skills—All our deals are just rubbish.

Numerate—We need someone who knows how to work in Excel.

Opportunities—Risks, or at least the chance to clear up someone else's mess.

Portfolio—We want you to do other things too, but we haven't thought of what they could be, so we thought this might make the job sound bigger than it really is.

Presentation skills—Because we're scared of PowerPoint.

Proven success—Success would be nice; maybe it will rub off on to us, too.

Reputation—Great, you've done it before.

Stakeholder—If we like you, we'll give you some shares—eventually.

Step up to the challenge—Because we can't.

Supportive—We need a brown-noser to tell us how great we are.

Team-building skills—We can't manage them, we need you.

The Bullshitter's Guide to Office Characters

Remember, the aim of the company bullshitter is to make him or herself look as good as possible in order to get promoted, get a raise, or just to be seen by the boss in the best light. Here are the bullshitter's victims and competitors, not forgetting those who inspire and those to suck up to.

Adequate/Inarticulate

Someone who is an expert at his or her job, but can't explain why or what actions should be taken without getting tongue-tied and frustrated.

Motto: I can't explain why, but it will work.

Articulate/Inadequate

A common sight in offices around the world, the Articulate Inadequate looks great and sounds great but in practice hasn't got a clue.

Motto: Looking good (usually while looking in the mirror).

Deceptionist

Good receptionists are worth their weight in gold to a company, but deceptionists will make everyone's life hell, requiring rewards almost every time they're asked to do something, however menial.

Motto: Over my dead body.

Hyperactive

Referred to as **hyper,** this person will rush around the office in a near panic while not actually achieving anything or doing any real work.

Motto: "It's a nightmare, oh my God!"

Influencer

This is the most subtle of individuals, having good **influencing skills** is essential to the bullshitter, it gets things done and gets you noticed.

Motto: Maybe I shouldn't say this, but . . .

Jobsworth

A widely hated figure, the jobsworth will do exactly what is required, or what they are contracted to do, no more and no less. They deserve all the abuse the bullshitter can muster.

Motto: It's not my job.

Journeyman

The journeyman will go from job to job, company to company without really achieving anything much. These types are happy being average, keeping their heads down and earning money in a quiet but generally efficient way.

Motto: Keep your head down.

Lame Duck

There's always a weakling who is picked on, someone who is a permanent victim and someone who the bullshitter uses as a stooge. A lame-duck manager is one who is covering a role for a while or who is on the way out.

Motto: Um, no thanks. OK yes, right.

Misery

People so long in the tooth and so unhappy in their work and their life that they cause disruption in any office. Often they haven't the wherewithal to leave or feel if they hang on a little longer they may get a pay-off.

Motto: Nothing works.

Motivator

This is the person (mainly men, it has to be said) who gets up in front of the team on a wet Friday morning in January and shouts "Whoa! Goood Moooorrrning!" and then to the muted response he says "What was that? I can't hear you!" while cupping a hand to the ear. His job is to "motivate the troops" and is generally quite useful to have around but mostly is just irritating. Motivators are usually unconsciously the biggest users of business bullshit, though they are not usually bullshitters.

Motto: Are you feeling good? (Said very loudly)

Movers and Shakers

The bullshitter's nightmare, people who actually do something, who make things happen. It is said that in a company of a thousand people the real work is done by about twenty people. They can be very senior or very junior, but they work like Trojans.

Motto: J.F.D.I. (Just Fucking Do It . . .) or *Leading from the front.*

Nerd

A useful bit part player in any bullshitter's life, the nerd knows technical things that bullshitters can use to find out information or make their own lives easier. The nerd is not necessarily a techie but just an expert or specialist; they're all the same to the bullshitter. The nerds themselves live in their own world, untouched by the machinations of business. They often refer to the people they support as "users."

Motto: I know, therefore I am.

Organizer

Someone who plans and organizes the office parties, charity collections, events, and anything else. That means they don't have to do their actual jobs.

Motto: Let me do that.

Players

To the bullshitter nearly everyone is a player, a competitor, someone to get or be aware of and someone to be used or stepped on for career gain.

Motto: Winning is everything.

Political Animals

The bullshitter is the archetypal political animal, using spin, lies, and deceit while pushing the image of overwhelming honesty to get to where they want to be.

Motto: Principles? What principles?

Scapegoat

Any bullshitter worth his salt will have a scapegoat lined up, whatever the situation.

Self-Toaster

Many offices have people who always say what they think, too honest to be aware of the consequences of their words, too decent to tell lies when it's needed. They are happy to score personal **own goals** if they think the situation demands it. The boss will tolerate it to a point but eventually they will go too far and they'll be sacked. This process is called self-toasting. The bullshitter will prime the self-toaster to his or her advantage, for selfish ends of course.

Motto: I'm right (that's the important thing).

Snake in the Grass, Spider in the Web

A key skill of the bullshitter is to rat on colleagues and friends. The snake will do it as a matter of course and the manager will love him or her for it. The spider is more manipulative but essentially the same.

Motto: Oh, what a tangled web we weave, when first we practice to deceive.

Stakeholders

Stakeholders put their neck on the line for a business or project; the stake may be financial or a reputation. Regardless, it's fodder for the bullshitter to exploit.

Motto: Show me the money!

Status Seekers

Those whose whole aim is to get to the next level in the management structure to improve their standing in the company. The bullshitter will take advantage of them, as being status seekers themselves they will know what it takes to get under their skin.

Motto: Profit without honor.

Team Player

Like the journeyman, team players will be happy playing their role in the team, with no leadership ambitions. The bullshitter will exploit the best of them in their team to make themselves look good.

Motto: For the team!

Wearer of Dead Men's Shoes

A manager so long in the job who does just enough to keep it and hold up the bullshitter's career progression. They are often themselves well practiced in the art of bullshit and for this reason are the ambitious bullshitter's worst enemy.

Motto: Thou shall not pass!

See also our section on management types on page 8.

BULLSHIT BINGO—Human Resources

PARTNER-SHIP	REDUNDANT	SUC-CESSION PLANNING	MIND-SET	HARMONY	APPRAISAL	RECRUIT-MENT POLICY	TEAM BUILDING	EXCITED
ONE TEAM	TEAM	SKILL SET	CAREER PLAN	HUDDLE	TOGETHER	VISION	CLARITY	ENERGY
PORTFOLIO	VIRTUAL TEAM	CHALLENGE	ATTITUDE	INTERPER-SONAL SKILLS	REPUTATION	GETS THINGS DONE	MOTIVATOR	NUMERATE
INNOVATIVE	ACHIEVE-MENT	LIFESTYLE	ASSESS-MENT	TEAM PLAYER	ABILITY	MENTOR	DYNAMIC	OPEN-DOOR
AWARE	COACH	CORE COM-PETENCE	STAKE-HOLDER	DOTTED LINE	CHECK IN	DOTTED LINE	OPPORTU-NITY	ORGANIZER

How to play: Simply check off 5 words or phrases in one meeting and shout out BINGO!

BULLSHIT BINGO—Managers Giving Career Advice

CARVE OUT A NICHE	CONVERT PLANS INTO ACTION	HIDDEN AGENDA	RESULTS-DRIVEN	YOU CAN DO IT IF YOU BELIEVE YOU CAN	YOU SCRATCH MY BACK AND I'LL SCRATCH YOURS	IT WILL BE THE MAKING OF YOU	GRAVITAS
WILL TO WIN	COMFORT ZONE	NO PRESSURE	TENACIOUS	HUNGRY	IT'S A JUNGLE OUT THERE	SINK OR SWIM	EYES AND EARS
HIT THE GROUND RUNNING	PROFILE	KNOWLEDGE	"NO" IS NOT IN MY VO-CABULARY	FAST TRACK	INCENTIVES	FINAL PIECE OF THE JIGSAW	DON'T ROCK THE BOAT
PROACTIVE	GRASP THE NETTLE	PRODUCE THE GOODS	GO THE EXTRA MILE	WORK ETHIC	LEARNING	PRIORITIZE	TIME MAN-AGEMENT
EYE ON THE PRIZE	FOOD CHAIN	QUID PRO QUO	WORK SMARTER	PROACTION NOT REACTION	SURVIVAL OF THE FITTEST	KNOW-HOW	LEAN AND MEAN
LONG HAUL	MANAGING EXPECTA-TIONS	ALIGNMENT	FREE RIDE	BANG THE DRUM	LEVELS OF HONESTY	ON THE MAP	OUTCOME

How to play: Simply check off 5 words or phrases in one meeting and shout out BINGO!

10. Planes, Trains, and Automobiles

Going to work for a large company is like getting on a train. Are you going sixty miles an hour, or is the train going sixty miles an hour and you're just sitting still?

—J. Paul Getty

Much management bullshit is derived from various modes of transport, which is a little weird but people seem to love using the analogies. It is catchy; just try it when next in a meeting. Mention something like "We could be cycling with no saddle here" and watch as the other attendees start wheeling out their favorite transport metaphors. There, you see even I'm doing it now.

Bumpy Ride
MEANING: A difficult time.
BULLSHIT: Usually caused by someone undermining the work in question.

Cycling with No Saddle
MEANING: Very uncomfortable.
BULLSHIT: Not really bullshit but everyone winces.

Deep Diving
MEANING: Detailed examination, in-depth analysis.
BULLSHIT: Brainstorming but supposedly with more thought and insight.

Drive
MEANING: Push, make sure things happen, passion, ambition.
BULLSHIT: People with drive are generally treated with some suspicion by colleagues, as they tend to be slightly scary.

Fast Lane, Fast Track
MEANING: Being in the fast lane means going faster than everyone else.
BULLSHIT: That's what they'd like you to believe, anyway.

Fine Tuning
MEANING: The finishing touches to a piece of work.
BULLSHIT: The final bit of added bullshit.

Flight Path, Flight Plan
MEANING: The route to take, how something such as a project is progressing.
BULLSHIT: Also referred to by some as the **journey**. Some just love this, talking about **navigational aids, turbulence, midair refueling, runway lights,** and **landings**— makes you want to throw up. **It will never fly** is the negative version.

Flying by the Seat of Your Pants
MEANING: Working using personal judgment and gut feelings rather than according to a predetermined plan.
BULLSHIT: Companies like to give the impression that they

are free-thinking and that they encourage risk takers; in reality, few will give too many personal freedoms.

Free Ride
MEANING: Getting a benefit at no cost.
BULLSHIT: For the bullshitter, there's always someone who will pay.

Get Out of First Gear, Get into Gear
MEANING: Accelerating, improving the speed at which something is done.
BULLSHIT: Used when something is stuck or not being done very fast. If a bullshitter is involved then there's a good reason why it's in the doldrums; either the bullshitter wants to show someone up or wants to get fired.

Going on Autopilot
MEANING: Doing something without conscious thought, staring into space, daydreaming.
BULLSHIT: Applies to most jobs that involve long hours at a computer. This could also be described as **going to screensaver.**

Green Light
MEANING: Go ahead.
BULLSHIT: Apparently some managers actually like to say "Give it the green light" or "Green light it" and they manage to keep a straight face.

Keep the Engine Running
MEANING: To keep something on hold with the expectation that when it begins again it needs to be up and running quickly.

BULLSHIT: Alternatively, keep something on hold until someone pays up, and then get out of there as fast as you can.

Park It
MEANING: Put it to one side until later.
BULLSHIT: The real meaning is "Put it to one side and don't mention it again" or "I'm too embarrassed to talk about that."

Radar
MEANING: To take notice, to get noticed.
BULLSHIT: Are you on the boss's radar? The bullshitter will be.

Reinvent the Wheel
MEANING: To create something that already exists.
BULLSHIT: As someone once said, "There are no new ideas, just old ones rehashed." Or something like that.

Road Map
MEANING: A bit like a **flight path** but less straightforward.
BULLSHIT: Another one to revel in, with **pit stops, barriers, detours, lay-bys**, and the odd **breakdown**.

Rocket Science
MEANING: Something incredibly complicated; usually used in the negative—"It's not rocket science, after all"—when referring to something simple that has been done poorly.
BULLSHIT: Well, except rocket science itself, nothing actually is rocket science, is it?

Tailspin
MEANING: Uncontrolled descent.

BULLSHIT: If this is being used, then something has gone drastically wrong. Time to enjoy the discomfort of others or just get your coat.

Up to Speed
MEANING: Fully informed.
BULLSHIT: The top bullshitter is always up to speed.

11. Sporting Bullshit and Clichés

Business is a good game—lots of competition and a minimum of rules. You keep score with money.

—Nolan Bushnell

Many managers in business borrow their sayings from sports, which often have their own specific language. Here are some common contributions that have found their way into our lives.

Ambassador (for the Game)
MEANING: A representative with authority.

BULLSHIT: Usually a player with some pedigree and a fair degree of gravitas; companies like to develop people who can play an ambassadorial role, usually dealing with trade organizations rather than doing any actual work.

Ballpark
MEANING: In the region of.

BULLSHIT: An imprecise term but one that most companies work with even if they like to think they are being accurate in their predictions.

Big-Game Temperament
MEANING: The ability to shine when under pressure or in the spotlight.

BULLSHIT: So your presentation was excellent and you defended your bad results with aplomb? You will go far.

Bystander, in the Audience, in the Crowd
MEANING: To stand by and watch the action.

BULLSHIT: "Are you in the stands watching the game or are you on the field as a player?" Oh, please!

Come of Age
MEANING: To grow up, mature, and gain independence. Young players mature from youth to experience usually in a particularly tough game, where they feature heavily and show their skills for the first time. Some maintain form, while most turn into **old lags** or **journeymen** or disappear never to be seen again.

BULLSHIT: In corporate culture this is usually applied to someone who, though young and previously anonymous, suddenly does a good piece of work or an excellent presentation. To the company bullshitter the person is a **clear and present danger** and must be dealt with.

Counterpunch
MEANING: From boxing, an attack, straight after your opponent has attacked.

BULLSHIT: The top company bullshitter will always have something ready to get back at a competing bullshitter.

Cover All Bases
MEANING: From baseball, to take everything into account.

BULLSHIT: The province of the conscientious company bull-shitter, who won't miss a trick.

Curveball

MEANING: From baseball, a tricky and unexpected problem.

BULLSHIT: Plenty of these in business without the help of your friendly neighborhood bullshit merchant.

Dream Team

MEANING: The best combination of team members.

BULLSHIT: Times are good, profits are high, there are no personnel issues, everyone on the team is performing very well; therefore it's a great team, a dream team. This is the time to start making changes before it all goes tits up.

Even Keel

MEANING: From yachting, keeping things steady and trouble-free.

BULLSHIT: At some stage in their careers every manager discovers that, like golf, sailing is the thing to get into if you want a promotion.

Final Score

MEANING: The result.

BULLSHIT: Imagine the managing director, having set the overly ambitious budgets and targets turning to the harassed finance team and saying, "So what's the final score?" Of course they know the figures are rubbish but self-preservation will prevail and they will give a favorable answer in the hope they can find something extra to **fill the gap**, during the year ahead.

Fire, Full-on, Passion, Pace, Pride, Total Commitment
MEANING: Passion, urgency, aggression, will to win.

BULLSHIT: Many play their sport with fire in the belly; a few managers use it as a management technique and when they do, most people just take the piss.

From Left Field
MEANING: From baseball, something outside the norm, unexpected.

BULLSHIT: Not a popular event with bullshitters, who like to be in control.

Game Plan
MEANING: The planned tactics for playing the game.

BULLSHIT: Everyone has one of these, one for doing your work and one for dealing with your colleagues.

Go for It
MEANING: Do it, with gusto.

BULLSHIT: Managers who "go for it" see themselves as great leaders; managers who encourage others with the term are usually great avoiders.

Goal
MEANING: From soccer, the target.

BULLSHIT: Goals are the lifeblood for ambitious managers everywhere. The company bullshitter will have goals too, aside from the publicly known ones.

Good Engine
MEANING: From car racing, lots of stamina.

BULLSHIT: Prepared to work late (probably with no pay).

Head Held High
MEANING: Proud, with dignity.
BULLSHIT: Usually the way to act when it all goes wrong.

Heavyweight
MEANING: From boxing, important, with gravitas . . .
BULLSHIT: . . . or just fat.

Hit the Ground Running
MEANING: Start something as if already experienced, after lots of preparation.
BULLSHIT: An impression you must give to your peers and managers.

Hungry
MEANING: Eager, keen, ambitious.
BULLSHIT: Even if they don't feel it, the bullshitter will always act it.

In with the Big Boys Now
MEANING: Playing with top teams or players, top companies, experienced and senior executives.
BULLSHIT: The implication is that they are much more important, mainly because of the direct relationship between money and importance, like nothing else matters.

Level Playing Field
MEANING: Everything being equal.
BULLSHIT: One of the great excuses: "It's not a level playing field, boss, so I can't include that in my budget . . ."

Monday Morning Quarterbacking
MEANING: Second-guessing.
BULLSHIT: Never try to second-guess a bullshitter.

Move the Goalposts
MEANING: To change the parameters and adjust targets.
BULLSHIT: If it doesn't look like they are going to hit their targets, bullshitters will change the rules or the parameters in their favor. Make sure you know who the bullshitters are; if they approach you with a proposal in the runup to **year-end**, make yourself scarce.

Next Level, Raise the Bar
MEANING: To improve performance from one perceived level to the next.
BULLSHIT: "If you can get to the next level, we'll give you a bonus, raise, better car, improved pension . . ." Yeah, right.

Plain Sailing
MEANING: From sailing, to finish with no complications.
BULLSHIT: Remember the parable about the swan looking serene on the surface while paddling furiously under the surface? Same thing.

Play Hardball
MEANING: From baseball and others, play it tough.
BULLSHIT: An impression some managers want to give, but in reality most are sneakier.

Played Out of Our Skins, Played with Their Hearts Out
MEANING: Worked so hard bits of body fall off or get exposed.
BULLSHIT: Not a pretty sight.

Pump Iron
MEANING: From bodybuilding, it's the buzz associated with heavy weight training.

BULLSHIT: Corporate use means "We're building up for a fight" or "building up the company" in some way.

Punch Above His/Her Weight
MEANING: From boxing, do better than expected or than one's abilities would suggest.

BULLSHIT: Very scary for the bullshitter who wants control and predictability.

Put Some Skin in the Game
MEANING: A euphemism for making an investment.

BULLSHIT: Sounds faintly disgusting, therefore is good bullshit. Possibly to do with leather balls, but can you imagine anyone really saying this?

Sea Change
MEANING: From sailing, a major change in the weather or state of the sea.

BULLSHIT: Initiating a sea change is a rare event; usually big changes happen by chance or when actions are delayed until it's too late.

Step Up to the Plate
MEANING: From baseball, be counted, take up the challenge.

BULLSHIT: Only for the naïve, foolhardy, or ambitious.

Sucker Punch
MEANING: From boxing, an unexpected successful attack.

BULLSHIT: Something the bullshit expert lives for.

Touch Base

MEANING: A term originating in baseball that has come to mean to verbally catch up with each other.

BULLSHIT: One of the most hated terms in business, and rightly so. It should be banned. Never say this to a British businessperson. It causes instant annoyance.

Where the Rubber Meets the Road

MEANING: From car racing, the time when something important happens or the point where something starts.

BULLSHIT: "All the preparation in the world counts for nothing until the rubber hits the road." Yuck!

Whole New Ball Game

MEANING: Some dramatic event that has changed the structure of the game.

BULLSHIT: Usually used to disguise the fact that someone has fucked up.

Winner

MEANING: The person who wins.

BULLSHIT: There is an obsession in business with being the winner, or to be seen as the winner. In the world of bullshit, the person who is perceived to be the winner may not necessarily be with person who has won.

World Class

MEANING: Outstanding, the best there is.

BULLSHIT: Managers who think they have a world-class team are generally self-deluded, lucky, or are due for a fall.

BULLSHIT BINGO—Sports

TOUCH BASE	HARDBALL	WINNER	STEP UP TO THE PLATE	RAISE THE BAR	SUCKER PUNCH	WORLD CLASS	MONDAY MORNING QUARTER-BACKING
AMBASSADOR	COUNTER-PUNCH	SEA CHANGE	GO FOR IT	EVEN KEEL	GAME PLAN	WHERE THE RUBBER MEETS THE ROAD	HEADS HELD HIGH
ON TRACK	BALLPARK	WHOLE NEW BALL GAME	PUMP IRON	DREAM TEAM	FINAL SCORE	PUNCH ABOVE HIS/HER WEIGHT	LEVEL PLAYING FIELD
BIG-GAME TEMPERAMENT	HUNGRY	GOAL	PUT SOME SKIN IN THE GAME	LEVEL PLAYING FIELD	PACE	BYSTANDER	TOTAL COMMITMENT
COVER ALL BASES	HEAVYWEIGHT	OUT OF THEIR SKIN	LEFT FIELD	GOOD ENGINE	PLAIN SAILING	FIRE	PASSION
CURVEBALL	COME OF AGE	NEXT LEVEL	IN WITH THE BIG BOYS	PRIDE	FULL-ON	FINAL SCORE	IN THE CROWD

How to play: Simply check off 6 words or phrases in one meeting and shout out BINGO!

12. Finance and Accounting

As long as people will accept crap, it will be financially profitable to dispense it.

—Dick Cavett

The world of finance and accounting is rife with bullshit words and phrases, but it's a boring world, so who can blame them for wanting to spice it up with a few colorful terms?

Financial People

The finance director or chief financial officer runs a company's finance department and apart from being responsible for **balancing the books**, they're there to criticize everyone else's work despite having no experience in any other job. Bizarrely many financial directors end up as the boss. **Bean counter** is a derogatory name for someone who works in finance and who apparently has little imagination; though in many ways they are the heroes of this section, keeping bean counters out of business generally seems like a good idea.

Bookkeepers and accountants tend to deal with facts and are generally bullshit-free, but don't expect a high-class lunch or a day out at the races; bagels with cream cheese and a meeting in the car park is more their idea of a day out. The most pedantic of finance people are those who would be inclined to pave over their front lawn because it's more efficient than gardening. They should be treated like bullshitters and be avoided at all costs.

Finance people call their data, spreadsheets, sales, or whatever they're working on "the numbers." It's a way of making them seem more important that they really are. Management will say things like "Your numbers look pretty good this week" rather than offer a proper compliment. When working on their data, the finance people will be **number crunching**, wanting to play up the grind that goes with working something out in detail. Accountants, bookkeepers, financially astute managers, and financial officers will always present every set of figures, every spreadsheet, and every P&L in the light that best suits them.

The preparation phase is crucial because every factor is looked at, numbers are rounded, stock written off or not included, and costs delayed. The common term for this is **massaging the numbers**. The next stage is **fine tuning**, which applies to the final details around a set of figures that have to be presented. So first the numbers have to be crunched, then massaged, and then lastly fine tuned. Insane but true, it's called **creative accounting**. In business, **creative accountancy** is the norm, especially when the company concerned is listed on the stock exchange and where excuses are needed and figures justified. **Aggressive accountancy** is associated with fraudulent accounting practice but often applies to companies that follow such rigorous financial policies that they forget about things like keeping customers happy, staff motivation, and strategy.

Budgets and Forecasting

For finance departments everywhere the favorite plaything is the **forecast**. They love them, the more the better, updating them endlessly, playing with the various permutations; they particularly enjoy making fun of the poor saps who put the forecast together in the first place. This leads to the **reforecast**, which is an update to the original forecast. As the trading year progresses, it's not unusual for corporations to be working with an original budget, a forecast 1, a forecast 2, and also year-on-year performance. Forecasting is all about guessing how much money will be taken in a given period of time; it's a great opportunity for bullshitters to fix their forecasts in such a way that it shows them in a good light.

Budget-setting follows the forecast and often ends up bearing little relationship to each other. The finance department will want to add in other **factors** and **overlay** extra business that they feel the original forecaster has missed. Then they will adapt their **template** (there's always a template) to make the final figure, which will then be adjusted further upward by the management.

Stretch targets are a favorite addition; there are those **targets** that everyone agrees on, and then there are those that just go a little further. The theory is that if everyone goes for the stretched target, then they'll beat the original ones. It never really works, because everyone knows what the real targets are and they'll work to them because it's easier. For bullshitters the only targets that matter are the ones they can crow about hitting. Occasionally a company will try to be experimental and decide to do without a budget, using different goals to stimulate their teams. This will only last about six months before a budget will be reintroduced and the **bean counters** can sharpen their pencils and go about justifying their jobs once more.

Financially astute bullshitters will use their own language to build a myth around their forecast, saying forecasting isn't **rocket science** or that they're not **robbing Peter to pay Paul** and that **problems are not solved by throwing money at them**.

Other classic phrases to watch out for are . . .

Above (or Below) the Line

MEANING: Above the line on a **profit and loss** statement is visible to everyone; below the line is not.

BULLSHIT: Shifting costs below the line is a canny way of boosting profits before tax. Taking costs above the line is a way of proving you are not a bullshitter and not open to classifying every unforeseen circumstance as **exceptional**.

Back End/Front End

MEANING: Back end is to put something off, for example it may be advantageous to budget sales targets toward the end of the financial year to make early sales look good against budget. A good trick if you know the first part of the year looks tricky, bad if you back end stuff and it doesn't come off. Front end is the opposite, when people bring things forward to their advantage.

BULLSHIT: The trick is to back end things then change jobs before the **shit hits the fan**, leaving the new guy to take the blame.

Back to Basics

MEANING: To return to a fundamental and uncomplicated way of doing something. Many companies say this when they've gone through a period of unsuccessful diversification.

BULLSHIT: Usually said when it's too late, by which time people will be saying that other immortal phrase, "They should have **stuck to their guns** . . ."

Bang for the Buck

MEANING: Determining which idea, task, project, or deal gives the best return on our time or investments.

BULLSHIT: Those who want to look good while going about it, ask which options give "the biggest bang for our buck" . . . and they're usually leaning back in the wobbly office chair with their hands behind their head, blessed with confidence that they actually look and sound good while saying it. Watch for telltale sweat patches—they're either lying or nervous.

Bread and Butter

MEANING: A livelihood, the usual way of making money.

BULLSHIT: There is nothing funny about this term. Expect that the user is probably pretty boring and on the financial team.

Building on Sand

MEANING: Not very stable.

BULLSHIT: Financial people and accountants' least favored emotion is lack of control. Here a plan or budget is agreed on without any basis of fact or substance behind the figures. It may shift considerably from the reality. Very uncomfortable.

Comparing Apples and Oranges

MEANING: Comparing two things that aren't alike.

BULLSHIT: Used by the bullshitters who are looking to defend their decisions by comparing figures that aren't really comparable.

Cost Effective
MEANING: "Is this worth our while?" A great term used to avoid doing any number of tasks, asking whether something is cost effective enables the user to delay while investigations take place.

BULLSHIT: Finance people will use this as a challenge, knowing that the challenged will not be able to prove the case either way.

Critical Path
MEANING: The critical path is a graphical description of a project or task with each step drawn up and accountabilities marked.

BULLSHIT: A classic, its great use is for making excuses, apportioning blame, and pointing to failure but very occasionally it actually works as intended.

Drawing a Line in the Sand
MEANING: A point at which no more money will be spent.

BULLSHIT: The line shall not be crossed, no more, no way . . .

Drivers and Levers
MEANING: The key elements that "drive" any business. So in retail they are sales, gross profit, stock, margin, and of course how much money can be screwed out of suppliers. The levers are the actions you take to manage the drivers. It make sense to them, if no one else.

BULLSHIT: The trick is to achieve a balance between them. Watch out for colleagues and companies that concentrate too much on one driver or pulling one lever too hard. It's a sign that the company strategy is wrong. Time to get your coat.

Exceptional
MEANING: Unforeseen, a one-off.

BULLSHIT: Normal but unforeseeable costs that management wishes to present as unrepeatable. In fact something exceptional happens every year.

Gap Analysis
MEANING: Looking into what was expected and what is real; a key part of any negotiation, with the gap being the difference between the two parties' expectations.

BULLSHIT: Analyze the gap? No, not that one, the one between your ears. . . . Why are you working in a place that talks about gap analysis?

Hand-over-fist
MEANING: Speedily, without control.

BULLSHIT: A good one for exaggerating problems. "We're losing money hand over fist."

In the Black/In the Red
MEANING: In the black is having money, while in the red is being in debt. While the latter is a common state of affairs to most of the public, it's an excuse for a dressing down in most companies. It's ironic that most people are more careful about their company finances than their own.

BULLSHIT: If you don't know the difference between being in the black or in the red, then you're in the shit.

Low-Hanging Fruit
MEANING: Self-preservation may keep you from laughing when this is used, especially when used without irony, but if your boss says to you that there is no low-hanging fruit in your department, take it as a compliment as it

means that there were no obvious opportunities to make easy or quick sales or cut costs.

BULLSHIT: This will be used to give the impression that the facts have been thoroughly investigated and no opportunities are available.

Magic Bullet

MEANING: In desperate times, when their forecasting has failed and they are far from hitting their budget, financial officers are known to prowl their business looking for a solution that will save them and their company—the so-called **magic bullet**. The poor, deluded fools.

BULLSHIT: The poor, deluded fools.

Overview

MEANING: Taking in the whole picture, reviewing the entire amount.

BULLSHIT: It's the financial officer's job to take an overview of the total company budget; it's the bullshitter's job to persuade the financial officer that more funds should be diverted to their projects and team.

Playing the Percentages

MEANING: The pick up strategy of most single men and coincidentally most product manufacturers and suppliers. The hopeful man will ask as many girls out as he can in the hope that one of them will say yes, while suppliers will produce as many types of products as they can, in the hope that one will sell and enable them to recoup their investment. Watch out for the phrase **"throw enough shit at a wall and some of it will stick,"** which has a similar use.

BULLSHIT: Playing the percentages is standard bullshitter practice regardless of the situation.

Pots of Gold

MEANING: Secret provisions, caches of money.

BULLSHIT: The company bullshitters keep these hidden from their boss during budgeting time so they can bring them in later to cover up any errors they may have made or if it looks like they won't hit their targets.

Profit and Loss, Bottom Line

MEANING: The **P&L** is the paper account of all costs and sales, but the crucial bit is the **bottom line,** finance speak for the profit left after all costs and expenditures have been taken into account. In other words, the *bottom line* of the profit and loss account statement.

BULLSHIT: When used by senior managers who want to know the "bottom line," what they are asking for is the answer without the bullshit. Therefore it's a great term to be heard using around the office.

Rubber Stamp

MEANING: Give authorization, a sign-off.

BULLSHIT: As long as someone else rubber stamps it, then that's fine—unless it's something the company bullshitter wants to take credit for.

The 80/20 Rule

MEANING: One of the greatest and most abused rules ever, derived from the work of Italian economist Vilfredo Pareto, his original observation being that 20 percent of the people had 80 percent of the wealth. This phrase has be hijacked and the theory applied to many aspects of business. For example, in retail 80 percent of sales come from 20 percent of the range; 20 percent of the stock takes up 80 percent of the available space; 80 percent of the work is done by 20 percent of your staff; and so on.

BULLSHIT: Fantastic for excuses and just the use of the name Pareto makes you sound intelligent even if you've no clue about him.

Top Line

MEANING: Sales or revenue, the top line of a P&L document.

BULLSHIT: **"Spare me the detail"** is a more common meaning these days, which of course leaves more scope for bullshit.

Transparency, Visibility

MEANING: Open, nothing hidden, usually to do with company results not hidden by spin or PR bullshit.

BULLSHIT: And if you believe that, you are a complete sucker.

Tweaking

MEANING: Slight adjustments.

BULLSHIT: Financial people always tweak figures right up to the last minute; it's in their nature and they can't help it.

Upside

MEANING: A benefit.

BULLSHIT: See **pots of gold**.

Wash Its Face (Does It?)

MEANING: Does it at least break even?

BULLSHIT: Another stupid expression, in response reply, "Yes, and it wipes its own butt as well." The management is bound to be impressed.

Corporate Bullshit

Here's some bullshit that's often applied by financial analysts to a company or by a financial officer to describe the situation they're in.

Acquisitions and Mergers

MEANING: Mostly because one company wants to buy another for the best price they can, they use terms like these to hide the fact that people are going to lose their jobs and that the company being bought will probably be decimated in the process.

BULLSHIT: Bullshit speak for takeovers.

Asset Stripping

MEANING: To ruthlessly sell the assets of a company after an acquisition.

BULLSHIT: No room for emotion, just make what you can and leave the carcass for others to clear up.

Basket Case, Hospital Case

MEANING: A term applied to an individual or company that looks like it's going under.

BULLSHIT: The chairman of a recovering company will say things like "In 1999 we were described as a basket case, and now look at us." This mantra will be repeated often in an effort to convince everyone that it's true, though in reality it often hides inept management. Avoid companies tagged with this unless they have sacked the management who were in charge at the time of the downturn. See **Cyclosis**.

Cherry Picking
MEANING: Choosing the best parts.

BULLSHIT: Picking and choosing those assets to buy in an acquisition and leaving the scraps with the vendor. This has achieved a wider meaning in management speak and is used throughout business.

Cyclosis
MEANING: The realization that the company success over a period of time has been completely due to cyclical factors outside of their control, such as a favorable economic cycle. Imagine presenting this one as a reason for your company's performance to the shareholders.

BULLSHIT: A great excuse in certain circumstances, especially for shifting blame.

Dead-Cat Bounce
MEANING: A small and temporary recovery in a market or trading sector following a large fall. Conjure up the image of a cat bouncing once after falling from a great height. He moves, but he's dead.

BULLSHIT: Not much worth as a bullshit term, as most people won't know what the hell you're talking about.

Double Dip
MEANING: An economist's term applied to a period where, for example, sales have been poor, but for a short while look good, but then go back to performing poorly again, usually for the same reasons as before.

BULLSHIT: The bullshitter using this will seem as though s/he knows his or her stuff, is always thinking about trends, and is good with **numbers.**

Enronomics

MEANING: After the Enron Company, this is now a description for a company where there is little in the way of proper accounting and fiscal techniques, probably managed by fools and bullshitters in combination.

BULLSHIT: Success depends on the staff being completely taken in by lies that are so big they couldn't possibly be true, and a finance team with no scruples. Watch your back. They will be looking for scapegoats.

Equity Victim

MEANING: Someone who, when he or she loses money on shares or investments, attempts to blame others for this loss. In reality it's his or her own stupid fault for investing in the things in the first place and believing the company bullshit.

BULLSHIT: For **Equity Victim,** read "sucker."

Gold Plating

MEANING: Much the way that cheap jewelry will masquerade as real, in the world of company takeovers, the company being bought deliberately overplays its value for a better price.

BULLSHIT: A recognized behavior of any bullshitter is to give something lots of benefits so that it appears better than it really is.

Green Shoots

MEANING: To show evidence of growth.

BULLSHIT: This is always mentioned after a company has gone though a tough time, usually after a **bloodbath,** when new management is desperate to find a good news story.

Open the Kimono
MEANING: To open the books to auditors, to expose something previously covered up.
BULLSHIT: Amazingly, some people actually use this term.

Seedcorn
MEANING: Start up funds, venture capital.
BULLSHIT: More bullshit is expended in getting money than almost anywhere—projections overstated, ambitions too high, and people being just plain greedy.

Slippery Slope, Downward Spiral, Tailspin, Freefall
MEANING: A fast descent.
BULLSHIT: Usually attributed to companies that are on the way to becoming a basket case, with share prices plummeting, never to recover.

Slush Fund
MEANING: A fund of money that isn't allocated to a specific thing or doesn't have a purpose.
BULLSHIT: Often illegal and often very handy in a tight corner.

Negotiations
Companies depend on good negotiators getting the right deal. It's bluff and double bluff, and there's no such thing as a win-win situation.

According to research and various training companies there are four major negotiation styles.

1. *Dealmaker*—obsessed by the deal, enjoys the process of horse trading (haggling) without much concern for the result
2. *Mediator*—likes to form a relationship, enjoys the personal side of negotiating but tends toward naïveté
3. *Fighter*—just wants to win no matter who is damaged
4. *Numerator*—can't deal with people or situations without figures at hand

We've added a fifth.

5. *Bullshitter*—chameleon-like skills, will be able to take on the persona of each of the above as needed, but won't make good negotiators; they lie too much and just complicate things because they don't really care about the deal, only about looking good.

Apparently most people have an element of each of these traits but some are more dominant than others. Here are some more terms for negotiations.

Bridge the Gap
MEANING: Any negotiator will tell you that a negotiation is about bridging the gap between two parties—it's a standard part of negotiation training.

BULLSHIT: Nowadays more synonymous with the gap between actual sales and the sales budget, commonly the boss (finger jabbing) will be saying *"You* promised me this, now what are *you* going to do to bridge the gap?" Negotiate your way out of that!

Bring to the Table, Lay Cards on the Table
MEANING: What's on offer or what is to be conceded.
BULLSHIT: Nothing much, generally.

Do a Number On
MEANING: To put one over, take advantage of, exploit.
BULLSHIT: Most negotiators, whether they admit it or not, want to put one over on their opposition.

Done Deal
MEANING: Finalized agreement.
BULLSHIT: It's all been agreed and there's no going back. Yeah, right.

Legs
MEANING: Lasting for a long time.
BULLSHIT: Most negotiators worth their salt negotiate an ending to a deal—usually after a year; it keeps them in their jobs.

Nail
MEANING: Finalize, complete.
BULLSHIT: Nailing a deal generally means to the advantage of the one doing the nailing.

Partnership
MEANING: Working together equally.
BULLSHIT: If a negotiator starts with the line "We want this to be a partnership," then you know that they really mean "We want you to believe it's a partnership, but really we want to exploit you."

Stake in the Ground
MEANING: State a specific position.
BULLSHIT: Someone has to make the first move in any negotiation . . . but where to put the stake?

Sunset, Sunrise Clauses
MEANING: Clauses—usually bonuses or termination dates—that are tied to the end or beginning of deals or contracts.
BULLSHIT: Usually they're not worth much, but the company bullshitter will always want to sneak a few clauses in just for fun if nothing else.

Unwind a Deal
MEANING: Renegotiate an agreement.
BULLSHIT: This can involve much groveling and great negotiation skills, as it sometimes indicates that some dickhead has made a mistake.

Up the Ante
MEANING: Increase the pressure by increasing a stake, refusing to agree to a deal or being tough.
BULLSHIT: Always risky, and company bullshitters hate taking risks.

Win-Win Situation
MEANING: A deal where everyone gets something good out of it—both sides win.
BULLSHIT: A deal where everyone thinks they're getting something good out of it, as both sides think they've won.

BULLSHIT BINGO—Finance

STRETCH TARGET	NUMBER CRUNCHING	BOTTOM LINE	DOWNSIZE	BUILDING ON SAND	STOCK	BACK END	FINE TUNING	OVERLAY	MASSAGE THE NUMBERS
BUDGET	BANG FOR THE BUCK	MOVE THE GOAL POSTS	WALL STREET	POTS OF GOLD	BENCH-MARKING	MAGIC BULLET	ENTREPRE-NEURIAL	FORECAST	80/20
PLAY THE PERCENT-AGES	THE NUM-BERS	TEMPLATE	FACTOR	SHARE-HOLDER VALUE	CASH FLOW	ROBBING PETER TO PAY PAUL	VISIBILITY	QUICK FIX	TIGHT
IN THE BLACK	IN THE RED	CASH NEUTRAL	GAP ANALYSIS	COST EFFECTIVE	QUICK AND DIRTY	DOUBLE DIP	INVESTOR	CRITICAL PATH	DRIVERS AND LEVERS
TIMING	DEVIL IS IN THE DETAIL	RESULT	LOW-HANGING FRUIT	REFORE-CAST	DOWN-WARD SPIRAL	RECOVERY	ABOVE THE LINE	SLIPPERY SLOPE	GREEN SHOOTS
COMPARE APPLES WITH ORANGES	BREAD AND BUTTER	ACTION	CHERRY PICKING	EXCEP-TIONAL	BELOW THE LINE	HOSPITAL CASE	BACK TO BASICS	UPLIFT	FREEFALL

How to play: Simply check off 6 words or phrases in one meeting and shout out BINGO!

13. I.T. Bullshit

Putt's Law

Technology is dominated by two types of people: those who understand what they do not manage, and those who manage what they do not understand.

The I.T. (information technology) department in most companies seems to be a very frustrating place. People appear to be condemned to installing systems that don't work and when they do work dealing with poor saps that have no clue how to run them.

It's no wonder that a phone call to the ubiquitous help desk leads to frustration, rudeness, and the odd gem of customer service when something is fixed by what seems a stroke of genius to the customer.

Omitting the ever-present jargon, here are a few I.T.-derived bullshit classics.

Access

MEANING: Right to enter.

BULLSHIT: I.T. people can get at information that others aren't authorized for. With this in mind, befriending the nerd is a good policy, especially when it comes to revenge.

Bandwidth
  MEANING: The amount of data that can be assimilated. A **low bandwidth** meeting is one that hasn't much content or scope; people with **narrow bandwidth** are considered too busy to cope. Either that, or they're just plain stupid.
  BULLSHIT: Bullshitters like to control bandwidth.

Connectivity
  MEANING: Ability to be connected.
  BULLSHIT: Hijacked by communicators and marketing people to show how in touch they are with their chosen targets, the company bullshit merchants will be concerned with connectivity to anyone they consider important.

Cut and Paste
  MEANING: Copy and transfer some information to someplace else, such as another document.
  BULLSHIT: Generally looks a bit slapdash.

Eating Your Own Dog Food
  MEANING: The process of using something that you have created and having the realization that it's rubbish.
  BULLSHIT: If only more managers were subjected to this process, what a nicer world we would live in.

Ego Surfing
  MEANING: Typing your own name into Google to see what comes back.
  BULLSHIT: In theory bullshitters will ensure that only good things come up when their name is typed in, but in reality it's one of the few things they can't control.

Firewall

MEANING: A barrier to prevent fire or attacks on your PC.

BULLSHIT: Managers who talk about firewalls to defend their company or department are generally referring to themselves.

Fuzzy Logic

MEANING: A form of math used to make decisions when information is imprecise.

BULLSHIT: A good term to use as a way of disagreeing with someone without calling them stupid.

Hand Holding

MEANING: To sit with someone while they complete an I.T. task.

BULLSHIT: Ah, bless them, but it can also used to describe any situation where someone is being helped through a task. It might be wise to ask why someone is being so helpful.

Hardwire

MEANING: To make something an automatic, integral part of the business.

BULLSHIT: The business guru will give guidance, a strategy will be formed, policies will be made, and a new way forward will be created for the company concerned. The new strategy and policies will become part of the company's culture and it will be hardwired in so that you don't forget it, buddy.

Integrity

MEANING: Stability and soundness of a system.

BULLSHIT: No matter how good the systems are, personal

integrity seems to disappear when the pressure is on and when personal ambitions come into play.

Intranet

MEANING: An internal Internet, with limited access.

BULLSHIT: In companies that use an intranet, each department generally has its own pages; a great chance to bullshit internally, but few people actually read them.

Jack In

MEANING: To log on.

BULLSHIT: Now used in this context "Can you jack in to the gray market and see what they're buying?"

Multitasking

MEANING: Doing several jobs or tasks concurrently.

BULLSHIT: Originally applied to processors, but now used with respect to people who are good at balancing several projects at once, which means they're usually female. See also **spinning plates** and **ball juggling**.

Ping

MEANING: To send an e-mail.

BULLSHIT: As a rule, people who say this are just annoying.

Portal

MEANING: A Web site that acts as a gateway to other Web sites, a doorway.

BULLSHIT: Another phrase borrowed by business to give the impression that more customers use them than they really do. This book is a portal for bullshit.

State of the Art
  MEANING: The most up-to-date technology, best in the industry.
  BULLSHIT: For many companies state of the art means a color printer or maybe a shredder, but for others it's that high-end system that costs a fortune and does nothing it was bought for.

User
  MEANING: Someone who uses a computer.
  BULLSHIT: Mainly a derogatory term for someone who has limited knowledge of how to work a computer. You have to say the word with a sneer to get the full effect.

Viral
  MEANING: Caused by a virus. In other words, spreads easily.
  BULLSHIT: Going viral is a sort of nirvana for many an ad agency, as it means success and bonuses all around.

Word of Mouse
  MEANING: Gossip by e-mail.
  BULLSHIT: This usually becomes second- or third-hand bullshit.

14. Acronyms

"My boss is like an OHP," he mused.
"An overhead projector?" she asked, a little puzzled.
"Yes, a little out of focus and a bit dim," he replied.

Where would American business be without acronyms? Every company has its own acronymic language, but here's a selection you'll hear often.

AAA
MEANING: Alive, Alert, Aggressive
BULLSHIT: This is how the company bullshitter wants to appear.

AFLO
MEANING: Another Fucking Learning Opportunity
BULLSHIT: One to use when the boss says "We must learn from our mistakes."

AKA
MEANING: Also Known As
BULLSHIT: The bullshitter, aka the promising candidate.

AKUTA
  MEANING: A Kick Up The Arse
  BULLSHIT: One for the boss.

APE
  MEANING: Attentive, Peripheral, Empathic
  BULLSHIT: Apparently this is about listening. Salespeople must be able to actually listen to their customers' needs rather than just go on about their products. Most of them nod attentively but really LOBNAH—lights on but nobody's at home.

ASTRO
  MEANING: Always Stating the Really Obvious
  BULLSHIT: A typical manager, then.

ATNA
  MEANING: All Talk, No Action
  BULLSHIT: A typical manager, then.

B2B
  MEANING: Business To Business
  BULLSHIT: Used by would-be Internet entrepreneurs in order to give the appearance of someone who knows about business.

BOGO
  MEANING: Buy One Get One (Free)
  BULLSHIT: Usually a sign that either the retailer or supplier is desperate.

BOHICA
  MEANING: Bend Over, Here It Comes Again

BULLSHIT: A permanent position for most workers, except brown-nosers who tend to adopt another position.

CADET

MEANING: Can't Add, Doesn't Even Try

BULLSHIT: This applies to most people who work in the finance department who are lost without Excel.

DINKY

MEANING: Double Income, No Kids Yet

BULLSHIT: Traditionally the richest group of consumers to be sucked up to.

DNA

MEANING: Building block, genetic make-up

BULLSHIT: Here the customer's DNA has nothing to do with his biological make up, nor has a company's DNA or a product for that matter. It all just makes you want to slap whoever is using this term.

DTS

MEANING: Danger To Shipping

BULLSHIT: What is it about some people in offices; they suddenly turn from attractive, young, vibrant individuals to dull, desk-bound fatties who in some countries would be classed as a shipping hazard.

DRIB

MEANING: Don't Read If Busy

BULLSHIT: Can't believe this is actually used, but it should be applied to nearly every bit of paper and e-mail ever received.

EDLP

MEANING: Every Day Low Pricing, a technique pioneered by supermarkets where they price products in such a way that it looks like they have squeezed every last penny on costs, in order to give the customer a better deal. So items normally priced at $5 will be priced at something like $4.83.

BULLSHIT: You can bet your life that some poor farmer in the third world is paying for the difference and not the supermarket in question.

FAQ

MEANING: Frequently Asked Questions

BULLSHIT: That the bullshitter always has an answer for.

FMCG

MEANING: Fast-Moving Consumer Goods

BULLSHIT: Something executives mention when they want to appear knowledgeable about retail and Wal-Mart in particular.

FNG

MEANING: Fucking New Guy

BULLSHIT: A reference to what a pain it is to train a new person in the office. But then you can give them all the shitty jobs, too.

FOBIO

MEANING: Frequently Outwitted By Inanimate Objects

BULLSHIT: Isn't it funny how the most calm, patient people can turn into psychopaths when it comes to adjusting their office chair.

FOC

MEANING: Free Of Charge

BULLSHIT: In the world of the corporate bullshitter, nothing is FOC.

FORCE

MEANING: Focus On Reducing Costs Everywhere

BULLSHIT: Accountants and new finance directors love to make a mark. They do this not by creating revenue but by cutting costs in the hope that everyone will work harder to make up the difference. Invariably in time this ruins the company.

FO

MEANING: Fuck Off

BULLSHIT: A good old-fashioned negotiation term.

FUBAR

MEANING: Fucked Up Beyond All Recognition

BULLSHIT: And the company bullshitter is nowhere to be seen.

FUCT

MEANING: Failed Under Continuous Testing

BULLSHIT: Applied especially not to something mechanical but to the poor sap who has started a job only to find that no one likes him.

GLAM

MEANING: Graying, Leisured, Affluent, Married

BULLSHIT: The fastest-growing consumer group in the Western world and the target of retailing bullshitters everywhere.

IMHO

MEANING: In My Humble Opinion

BULLSHIT: Well, it's not humble at all, is it? To be lumped in with the classic "with all due respect."

IPATTAP

MEANING: Interrupt, Patronize, Argue, Threaten, Terminate, Apply Penalties.

BULLSHIT: This is presumably what passes for customer service in the banking industry.

JFDI

MEANING: Just Fucking Do It

BULLSHIT: Funnily enough, it's much more satisfying to actually say the words rather than the acronym.

KAS

MEANING: Knowledge, Attitude, Skills

BULLSHIT: The bullshitter will prefer Cunning, Aptitude, Shitting-on.

KISS

MEANING: Keep It Simple, Stupid

BULLSHIT: One of the most patronizing acronyms, so therefore one of the most used.

KPI

MEANING: Key Performance Indicators—the lifeblood of any financial manager—enable them to monitor how the business is performing against a set of predetermined criteria. Many businesses, when they discover the joys of using KPIs, go crazy, overusing them and putting their staff under strain.

BULLSHIT: The trick is to make sure KPIs are attainable and will never be threatened. If that looks likely, someone else will get the blame.

KVI

MEANING: Known Value Item, a line in a supermarket that everyone knows the value of, e.g., bread, milk, condoms . . .
BULLSHIT: Most retailers kid themselves about what a KVI is. Most suppliers dream of getting a KVI especially if they are the only ones who supply it.

LANO

MEANING: Lights Are Not On
BULLSHIT: And no one is home, except the ubiquitous bullshitter.

LAST

MEANING: Listen, Advise, Solve, Thank
BULLSHIT: A way to deal with problems, bless them.

MILE

MEANING: Maximum Impact, Little Effort
BULLSHIT: The bullshitter's motto, or one of them anyway.

MMM

MEANING: Measurable, Manageable, Motivational
BULLSHIT: Yawn . . .

NB

MEANING: No Bullshit
BULLSHIT: No entertainment.

NFG

Meaning: No Fucking Good
Bullshit: One that should be used more often.

NMFB

Meaning: Not My Fucking Business
Bullshit: A classic work-deflection tactic.

PANIC

Meaning: Pressured And Not In Control
Bullshit: A good description for most managers.

PDQ

Meaning: Pretty Damn Quick
Bullshit: Not used much these days, but effective anyhow.

PEBCAK

Meaning: Problem Exists Between Chair And Keyboard
Bullshit: As ever a bad workman blames his tools.

PICNIC

Meaning: Problem In Chair Not In Computer
Bullshit: These I.T. ones are just so witty.

POS

Meaning: Piece of Shit
Bullshit: To some this means Point of Sale, but we like this
    version, with the alternative being BOS, for Bag o' Shit—
    basically the project that has gone wrong.

PPPP (The Four P's)

Meaning: Product, Price, Promotion, Place

BULLSHIT: One of the retail basics, although real-estate agents seem to have adopted it as part of their bullshit.

RTFM
MEANING: Read The Frigging Manual
BULLSHIT: Another one from those helpful guys in the I.T. department.

SNAFU
MEANING: Situation Normal, All Fucked Up
BULLSHIT: Implying that everything is a mess, all the time.

SSDD
MEANING: Same Shit, Different Day
BULLSHIT: Depressing or what? Anyone saying this deserves all they get.

SWOT
MEANING: Strengths, Weaknesses, Opportunities, Threats
BULLSHIT: Analysis technique beloved by consultants everywhere.

TEAM
MEANING: Together Everyone Achieves More
BULLSHIT: When this is said, the speakers usually have their fingers crossed behind their back and are probably thinking "Because then I don't get the blame."

TFL
MEANING: Too Fucking Late
BULLSHIT: Time for reprisals and **blamestorming**.

TINA

MEANING: There Is No Alternative

BULLSHIT: For most bullshitters, this doesn't apply; they usually have their **exit strategy** all worked out.

TQM

MEANING: Total Quality Management

BULLSHIT: A blast from the past, management guru jargon from the eighties. It's included because I miss it and its associated bullshit.

WOMBAT

MEANING: Waste Of Money, Brains, And Time

BULLSHIT: Applies to many.

WYGIWYD

MEANING: What You Get Is What You Deserve

BULLSHIT: Yep, absolutely. Although the bullshitter will never think so.

WYSIWYG

MEANING: What You See Is What You Get

BULLSHIT: People who tell you that this applies to them are lying.

YOYO

MEANING: You're On Your Own

BULLSHIT: Useful when avoiding blame. Sometimes **YOYOB**: You're On Your Own, Buddy.

BULLSHIT BINGO—Acronyms

JFDI	TEAM	TINA	SSDD	KISS	FMCG	MILE
EDLP	YOYO	TQM	PDQ	ASTRO	DINKY	PEBCAK
AKA	WYSIWYG	WOMBAT	PANIC	FO	DTS	POS
PICNIC	AAA	MMM	LANO	KAS	FUCT	TFL
SWOT	FNG	RTFM	LAST	KPI	DNA	RTFM
SNAFU	AFLO	KVI	AKUTA	FORCE	FAQ	PPPP

How to play: Simply check off 5 acronyms in one meeting and shout out BINGO!

15. The Weird and Wonderful

People that are really very weird can get into sensitive positions and have a tremendous impact on history.
—Dan Quayle

Here's a selection of the oddest and most eccentric phrases that we just couldn't categorize. It seems that corporate types compete to see who can come up with the strangest and most exotic terms. We have a term of our own for those people: fuckwit.

Assmosis
MEANING: From the *Dilbert* cartoon, a description of the process by which a person climbs the career ladder by sucking up to the boss.
BULLSHIT: So a good bullshit technique, then.

Bo Derek
MEANING: The perfect deal.
BULLSHIT: This was named after the actress who appeared in the 1979 film *10*. Seems a bit out of date now. Maybe now it should be a Britney or a Christina or a Pamela . . . maybe not.

Checking the Pulse, Finger on the Pulse
MEANING: How things are progressing, the state of play.
BULLSHIT: All businesses have a heart and can be likened to an organism, so this is a logical term; unfortunately bullshitters have no heart.

Chinese Walls
MEANING: A term originated from the 1929 stock crash where an imagined wall is put up; when information trading is prohibited because of mutual interest. Say, between two companies owned by an umbrella company.
BULLSHIT: You can almost guarantee it's a complete sham, especially when stakes are high.

Cooking with Gas
MEANING: Under way, making rapid progress.
BULLSHIT: What the hell is this all about? Often said by managers who feel something is on the way to being a success. "Now we're cooking with gas!" Why not electricity or microwaves or nuclear power? Maybe gas just sounds hotter.

Dog's Bollocks
MEANING: From the premise that a dog is so fond of licking its bollocks, it follows that there must be something pretty bloody good about them. So this phrase actually means something outstanding.
BULLSHIT: A favorite of British senior managers who want to appear "one of the boys."

Emperor's New Clothes
MEANING: From the Hans Christian Andersen fairy tale. In this context it comes into play when someone convinces

themselves that the value of a valueless object is very high. Also applies when a leader follows a hopeless path with his team backing him, even though they all know it will end in failure.

BULLSHIT: Pretty common throughout the corporate world, only in business you don't get a small child pointing out the obvious failings.

Going Postal

MEANING: Going insane, especially after something bad happens.

BULLSHIT: Postal workers in America were prone to losing it in a big way because of the stress associated with their jobs. Posting letters is stressful, is it? Yeah, right.

Herding Cats

MEANING: Impossible.

BULLSHIT: Try it and you'll understand.

Mad as a Box of Frogs

MEANING: Unpredictable, totally chaotic.

BULLSHIT: Excellent term that applies to most offices and work situations that involve many departments in a large business.

Pear-Shaped

MEANING: Gone wrong.

BULLSHIT: There doesn't seem to be an obvious origin for this term except that maybe something that was meant to be circular went pear-shaped. Of course bullshit comes into play when it becomes obvious that plans are going wrong.

Pigs Might Fly
  MEANING: It won't happen, extremely unlikely.
  BULLSHIT: A term that becomes common around bonus
    time.

The Proof Is in the Pudding
  MEANING: Don't assume anything.
  BULLSHIT: Good advice all around; bullshit is everywhere.

Put This One to Bed
  MEANING: Finish off, everything dealt with.
  BULLSHIT: The implication is that those involved should
    move on to something else; many are so eager to go on to
    the next project it becomes a good opportunity to bury
    anything unwanted in the last project.

Run It Up the Flagpole (and See If It Gets a Salute)
  MEANING: To test something to see if it works or gets ap-
    proved.
  BULLSHIT: It was crap to start with, if no one notices how
    crap it is then we'll put it into production.

Salmon Day
  MEANING: One of those days when it feels like you're swim-
    ming against the current only to get screwed, then die at
    the end.
  BULLSHIT: Too many of these and it's time to go, change
    jobs, change your life, change countries.

Smoke and Mirrors
  MEANING: Generally something ephemeral that hides the
    true situation.

BULLSHIT: A bullshitter, the spin doctor, and the PR people—it's all smoke and mirrors, really.

Stick It in the Rocket and Blast Off
MEANING: Aggressively start a project once everything is in place.

BULLSHIT: Could you say this in a meeting with a straight face? Avoid anyone who can.

Talk Until Blue in the Face
MEANING: An attempt to persuade someone of something for a long time, with no result.

BULLSHIT: Occurs in most meetings.

Ticking Time Bomb
MEANING: A disaster waiting to happen.

BULLSHIT: It's amazing how many there are when you look for them. The accomplished bullshitter will be aware of what the major upcoming issues are and will instigate the problem, either to undermine the boss or solve said problem, becoming a hero in the process.

Tongue in Cheek
MEANING: Something humorous said in a serious way.

BULLSHIT: The worst part is when you think it's something said tongue in cheek only to discover they meant it. Particularly bad if it's your boss.

Up His or Her Own Ass
MEANING: Pretentious, self-important.

BULLSHIT: Yep, there are plenty of these people around, mainly chefs, marketing people, and authors.

Whistling Past the Graveyard

MEANING: Ignoring a serious or impending problem while knowing it's really there all the time.

BULLSHIT: A constant theme through company life; many problems never get addressed until it's too late—bullshit rules.

BULLSHIT BINGO—The Weird and Wonderful

SMOKE AND MIRRORS	WHISTLING PAST THE GRAVEYARD	UP HIS OR HER OWN ASS	PUT THIS ONE TO BED	STICK IT IN THE ROCKET AND BLAST OFF	RUN IT UP THE FLAGPOLE	DEEP DIVING
GOING POSTAL	TONGUE IN CHEEK	FINGER ON THE PULSE	EMPEROR'S NEW CLOTHES	PROOF IN THE PUDDING	MAD AS A BOX OF FROGS	COOKING WITH GAS
DOG'S BOLLOCKS	CHINESE WALLS	ASSMOSIS	HERDING CATS	PIGS MIGHT FLY	TICKING TIME BOMB	BIG ASK
BANG FOR THE BUCK	BO DEREK	STRETCH THE ENVELOPE	SALMON DAY	BALLS IN THE AIR	SQUARING THE CIRCLE	STICK TO THE KNITTING
DOG AND PONY SHOW	TITS OUT	BLAMESTORM	LOW-HANGING FRUIT	PEAR-SHAPED	TALK UNTIL BLUE IN THE FACE	EATING YOUR OWN DOG FOOD

How to play: Simply check off 5 in one meeting and shout out BINGO!

16. Playing Hooky

Far from idleness being the root of all evil, it is rather the only true good.

—Søren Kierkegaard

Bullshitting isn't all about ambition, screwing others, and getting to the top on their backs. It can also include excuses and crap from those fakes at the other end of the spectrum, the mentally lazy and physically idle.

Recently it was shown that American workers are outstanding at this aspect of work and by their efforts can extend nonwork time by up to fourteen days a year. Here are some ways of wasting time and slacking off.

1. The cigarette break. This involves finding five minutes several times a day, usually outside or in a designated area to smoke, while nonsmoking colleagues carry on working. Nonsmokers can pretend to smoke and go for the breaks anyway.
2. Men's rooms are often packed with suitable reading material just for the occasion that often warrants a half an hour's break—a good crap.
3. Passing the baton. You are given work to do; you can either ignore it or pass it on to someone else, saying that you were asked to hand it to them.

4. Feigning illness, a classic and the most obvious trick. In the last decade it was backache, but these days it's stress, which is much less measurable and sometimes, if a bullshitter has a hand in it, actually genuine.

5. If approached with some work, ask for a specific form or proof that it's been authorized. Put other people's initials on documents handed to you and pass them on.

6. Checking out the competition is often a good excuse for a trip abroad or at least to somewhere nicer than the workplace.

7. Create a problem or a crisis; spend all day "sorting it out."

8. Saying "I don't know how that works" or "I'm not trained in that" is a good standby, as is pretending to be stupid or just keeping quiet.

9. Working from home. This is especially good if you can get your boss to agree to you taking a regular working-at-home day. "It's amazing how much I get done when there are no distractions."

10. Being aware of who generates the work. Plan your route to your desk so that you avoid them. Try to situate yourself in such a way that you can't be seen. Do just enough work to pass the minimum standard required.

11. Ensure that your computer screen is not seen by anyone; this will enable you to spend days surfing (make sure you go through Google rather than type directly into the Web browser; it's less likely to be picked up), playing games, gambling, trading on eBay, and e-mailing friends.

12. Working lunches and coffee breaks are always extendable and difficult to check up on. Just don't go back to the office if you're too drunk or high.

13. Work is often so boring that it induces sleepiness, and you may find the need for a doze. The restroom can be busy and uncomfortable, so find someplace cozy, such as under your desk, but take an object with you such as a pen. Then if you're woken up by someone, you can be just looking for the pen you'd "dropped" earlier.

THE LAST WORD

I hope that this book has given you some insight into the world of the company bullshitter and given you some laughs along the way.

Using this type of terminology isn't a crime; it may help you get that promotion that you've always deserved. We all use it unconsciously and consciously, but when it turns malicious and people start getting hurt it's time to consider your options.

You have to question whether you want to play the game seriously or not. You should ask yourself these questions:

1. Can I take regular criticism and unpopular actions, without remorse?
2. Can I cope with having double standards?
3. Can I sleep at night without feeling guilty about my actions?
4. Can I live with being a liar throughout my working life?
5. Are money and success more important than feeling good about myself?
6. Am I more important than the company I work for and my colleagues?

7. Can I act in a way that is at odds with my personality as long as it gets the result I want?
8. Can I suck up to important people without embarrassment?
9. Can I present myself with aplomb, whatever the situation?

If you answered yes to all of these then you're likely to be a first-class bullshitter.

If you answered no to any of them and yes to some, then you may not make it as a bullshitter. You'll be compromised at some stage, but if you can live with it and brazen it out then you'll probably succeed.

For those who answered no to all these, then you're obviously a nice person. Your main issue is going to be about how you can avoid becoming a bullshitter's victim. Hopefully this book will help, but just for you, here are the main five ways to spot a liar:

1. Failure to make eye contact. You may find the inexperienced liar looking away as they speak, but the trick to look for is the liar looking at the spot between your eyes rather than directly at them.
2. The liar's voice changes, fluctuates, or he speaks too quickly, in a rush to get the sentence out.
3. The liar shifts position as she speaks, becomes unusually fidgety.
4. The liar covers or puts a finger over his mouth or touches her nose, however briefly. Especially if they haven't done it before, it could signal that a lie is being told.
5. If you see the liar pulling his collar or scratching his neck, it shows anxiety and it's worth questioning their motives further.